igni

# OFFEN

## cross-driven mission

# DAI HANKEY

Foreword by Andy Hawthorne

GO//PREACH//PRAY//LOVE//LIVE//NOW

Version 1.0. First published in the United Kingdom in 2008.

ISBN: 978-0-9560648-0-6

Cover and book design by:
STØRM Visual Communications Ltd.
stormvc.co.uk

Book production for the publisher by,
Bookprint Creative Services, <www.bookprint.co.uk>
Printed in Great Britain.

THIS BOOK IS DEDICATED TO
EVERY CHRISTIAN WHO EVER TOOK
A RISK, A KICKING OR A BULLET FOR JESUS.

# CONTENTS:

What others said about this book ....................................................... ii

Acknowledgements ....................................................... iv

Foreword by Andy Hawthorne ....................................................... vi

Intro ....................................................... vii

CHAPTER ONE: CROSS-DRIVEN MISSION ....................................................... 1

CHAPTER TWO: SHOUT OUT! ....................................................... 23

CHAPTER THREE: FIGHTING ON OUR FACES ....................................................... 51

CHAPTER FOUR: FUEL FOR THE FLAMES ....................................................... 71

CHAPTER FIVE: RIGHTEOUS REVOLUTION ....................................................... 95

CHAPTER SIX: ....................................................... 115

References ....................................................... 126

Ignite Declaration ....................................................... 132

# WHAT OTHERS SAID ABOUT THIS BOOK:

Dai Hankey's heart is really transparent as he lays it all out in Offensive: Cross Driven Mission. It's an uncomplicated primer getting into why we must do whatever it takes to get the Gospel out there.
**- BILL WILSON** *[Pastor & Founder Metro Ministries]*

What we want is books written by people who live out daily what they are writing about. This book is exactly that, because Dai Hankey is exactly that, a true disciple with a heart that burns for the lost. This book is not about filling you with ideas, but more about setting your heart on fire to see your generation reached, and if even a tiny amount of Dai's zeal rubs off on you, then you had better get ready for what will inevitably follow!
**- TIM CHESHIRE** *[Superhero]*

When we were looking to appoint someone to front the evangelism and discipleship arm of Ignite there was only really one person for the job – Dai! He lives and breathes the good news of Jesus and has a God-given ability to connect with young people. Offensive has been transformational for many teenagers in Wales, and this book will no doubt be transformational in the lives of those who read it.
**- NIGEL JAMES** *[Ignite/Third Day Road Pastor]*

I have known Dai for many years and it has been a thrill to see his passion for God, his passion for a true presentation of the Gospel and his passion regarding the lostness of the lost, especially amongst the youth. I have spent time over a good number of cups of coffee hearing Dai talking about raising up a 'Radical Generation' of Christian Young People who are not afraid of 'The offence of the Cross'. As I read the pages of the book I could hear Dai speaking, his passion coming through. Dai has remained being who he is – a great Welsh character, so as to be more effective in reaching today's generation. As an evangelist myself, eager to communicate Christ, I heartily recommend this book as a practical down to earth writing, earthed in experience.

- **PETE HODGE** *[OAC Evangelist]*


Rarely have I read a book which so clearly reflects the personality of its author, but if you have met Dai Hankey you will soon know that this book was not written by a ghost writer. This is Dai at his most passionate, pleading for reality and consistency in our Christian walk. The way he expresses himself may be different from you and me, but what he says is like a pep pill to kick start us into living wholeheartedly for the Lord, who gave Himself for us. Read and like me be challenged. Be very challenged!

- **ROGER CARSWELL** *[Evangelist and author]*

# OFFENSIVE ⊙

# ACKNOWLEDGEMENTS

Quite simply this book would never have happened without the encouragement of all the guys at Ignite, especially my boss and good friend Gary Smith. Thanks for bearing with me mate. Also thanks to Nigel James for his insightful feedback and help in editing my rambled writings. Big thanks also to The Evangelization Society (TES) for getting behind the vision of Offensive and helping to fund the running of the course here in South Wales. To Andy Hawthorne, thanks a million for taking me seriously enough to write the foreword and for being a good mate and encouragement to me over the years. Similarly, to Bill Wilson, Tim Cheshire, Roger Carswell and Pete Hodge thanks for your endorsements – cheques are in the post!

Nuff Respect to the crew at Christchurch (Newport) for lending me an office and hooking me up to their wi-fi to finish chapter 3, and also to Dan Clemo of STØRM Visual Communications Ltd. for his graphical design genius, coffee and pizza! I've also got to express deep gratitude to Jeff and Jen Taylor for opening up their home to me and keeping me topped up on coffee while I finished the last few chapters. God bless you guys.

Another shout out that's just got to be made is to the hundreds of young people in Cardiff and beyond who have now done the Offensive course, put up with my crazy rants and scoffed all my donuts! Your commitment, energy and passion for the gospel are what it's all about. You're the future right now and you're such an inspiration and encouragement to me. God bless you. To my Offensive Freeloaders – Beacher, Stevey Scott, Beci and Edith – you're immense and I just see Jesus in you. Thanks for being part of it all!

I can't write my acknowledgements without expressing huge love and gratitude to my lush wife Michelle, for wearing my ring, sticking by my side, coping with my absent mindedness as I pondered on different bits of the book, and for generally supporting, praying, and looking after me. I love you so much sweets – thank you. In the same way I've got to also thank my beautiful kids Elen and Josiah for making my home so special and full of fun – you're so precious to me and are such worthy distractions!!!

Above all, thanks to Jesus Christ for saving me, and letting me be part of your big, cross-driven adventure. I love you forever. I hope this book makes you smile and gives you glory.

*Dai*

# OFFENSIVE 🔥

## FOREWORD BY ANDY HAWTHORNE

❝ By nature I'm an evangelist, the type of guy who likes to go fishing with a big net and chuck lots of fishes into the Church where the poor pastors have to cope with the fact that they flip flop around and that some of them, to be honest, stink the place out. I know I can be a bit annoying in my constant exhorting to get fishing but, as I've grown a bit older I think I've learnt to appreciate the awesome work that pastors of local Churches do, and I have learnt that we are not going to get anywhere without pastors and evangelists working hand in hand.

What I really love about Dai Hankey is that he is that rare beast – an evangelist with a pastor's heart. He longs to see young people come to Christ and works so hard to see that happen, but he is also passionate to see those young people released into effective mission themselves. That is not only unbelievably important, but simply the only way we are going to get the job done.

You check back through history and right from the word go it has been radical sold out missional young people who have been at the heart of every big move of God. Right from the start on the shores of Lake Galilee when Jesus called his own youth group (that's right – according to historians the disciples were between the ages of 14 and 22 when he called them) to today in China where the revival movement is being spearheaded by teenagers: it has been cross driven young people who have been at the forefront of what God's up to.

That's why Dai has written this wonderful little book with the deep desire that young people in Cardiff and across the UK and, who knows, right across the world will get in on the action, join the revolution and start to "step into the mess and save the day."

Don't you just like the sound of that?  ❞

In the same way that the Nintendo Wii sounds more like a bodily function than the ground-breaking games console that it actually is, I guess I could have come up with a slightly more helpful title for this book than 'Offensive' – a name that seems to confuse and intimidate as many people as it attracts and inspires. However, you've successfully managed to navigate your way past the front cover, so nice one for being brave/intrigued/stupid/bored (delete as appropriate) enough to give it a go. Seeing as this is the introduction bit, it probably makes sense for me to try to explain what the whole 'Offensive' thing is all about, so here we go...

Basically the Bible tells us that the cross of Jesus was, is and always will be 'offensive'[1], yet incredibly it is the way that God chose to step into our mess and save the day. Jesus' rescue mission was cross-driven, and so it should come as no surprise that the mission, message and life that He has called us to pursue is also inspired and driven by the cross.

Jesus carried His cross to save the world, and He calls us to do the same! [2]

Back in 2005 I started working for Ignite as their Evangelism and Discipleship Coordinator, and one of the first things that I did was set-up a series of evangelism training sessions for young people in Cardiff that made a big deal of the cross. For better or worse I called it Offensive: Cross-Driven Mission.

Rather than offering yet another take on the freshest, flashest and most effective ways of 'doing mission', Offensive sought to be more broad in its approach, recognising that what works well in one culture or context may be completely ineffective in another. By considering the life, example and sacrifice of Jesus, Offensive seeks to explore the stuff about evangelism that's non-negotiable and applies to us whoever and wherever we are: The call to mission, the message we've got to shout about, the power of prayer, the role of love, and the impact of a life that backs up the words we speak.

# OFFENSIVE ⟳

Offensive is all about raising up an irresistible army of cross-driven young people who are sold out for Jesus and have been gripped and equipped by His immense soul-saving, life-changing, world-shaking good news message. This book has been written with a deep conviction that the gospel is the only hope for our mashed-up world, and that we all have a part to play in getting it out there! I truly believe that when God's people stop messing around and actually pour all their energy, emotion, courage and prayer into reaching the lost, preaching the gospel with compassion, and living like it matters, then the devil starts filling his pants and God starts doing big stuff.

Now I've got to confess that I'm much more comfortable preaching this stuff in a room full of sweaty, Jesus-loving young people than I am trying to write it down as a book. I'm better with a mic than a Mac! Therefore it won't take you long to realise that a South Wales Valley boy with a dangerous caffeine addiction doesn't quite write in a conventional way. I guess I'm a freak! My point is this – if my writing style is offensive to you then I'm sorry, and I just ask that you would try to roll with it as best you can. I assure you that my motives are pure and I'm not a psycho. However, if the actual content (i.e. the Gospel and its implications) offends you, then I can't apologise for that, because I didn't write it – God did! I just pray that as you read through these pages you'll see the sheer beauty, mercy and urgency of the cross of Jesus in a fresh way.

I haven't written this book to try to impress anybody or make a name for myself (I mean why would anyone with a crazy name like mine want to be famous?!) Rather I simply want to play my part in unleashing a generation who are so passionate about the name of Jesus, that they will give everything and stop at nothing to reach and rescue the lost, broken world that He died for.

I pray from the bottom of my heart that this book will challenge, change, bless and inspire you as you step out in faith to play your part in the awesome cross-driven mission that Jesus has set before us.

And may God get all the glory for it!

*Dai*

# CHAPTER ONE

## CROSS-DRIVEN MISSION

"SEND ME,
I'LL GO, LEMME GO!" [3]

**- LECRAE**

# OFFENSIVE ⚡

## SO OTHERS MAY LIVE

On a sunny 1960's summer afternoon in Wales, on the banks of the river Ystwyth (try saying that with a mouth full of mushrooms!) a young girl slipped off the river-bank and got sucked straight down to the bottom of the river, where she started to drown. As people nearby started to freak out, a brave young student dived in to save the day, but despite her courage, she too was soon sucked down! As the panic started to escalate, a man in a canoe further up the river heard the screams, paddled down, dived in and dragged them both to safety.

I'm quite glad he did too, because the bloke in the canoe was my dad, and the student was my mother! If he hadn't saved her life that day, they'd have never got married, I'd never have seen the light of day and you wouldn't be reading this book right now!

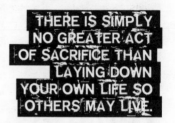

THERE IS SIMPLY NO GREATER ACT OF SACRIFICE THAN LAYING DOWN YOUR OWN LIFE SO OTHERS MAY LIVE.

Life-savers are heroes. But what is it that drives such people to throw themselves in the way of danger and risk their lives in such incredible ways? The motto of the US National Coastguards says it all:

*"So Others May Live."*

In short – people are precious and worth saving no matter what the cost! There is simply no greater act of sacrifice than laying down your own life so others may live.

## GOD TO THE RESCUE

You don't need to be the sharpest tool in the box to recognise that our world is drowning. People all around us are sinking in fear, despair, heart-break and pain, crying out for someone to rescue them. Tragically, so many are looking in all the wrong places and trying all the wrong stuff to escape – cash, careers, drugs, casual sex, but rather than saving them – it only drags them down deeper. Let's face the facts – humanity needs a hero more than it ever did, as Bono so poignantly wrote:

**JESUS IS THE FLESH AND BLOOD EVIDENCE THAT GOD'S HEART BEATS FOR LOST PEOPLE!**

*"Jesus can you take the time to throw a drowning man a line?"* [4]

That lyric perfectly captures the heart-cry of so many people on planet earth right now: *"God, if you're there, can you please do something to help us? We're dying down here!"* God's not oblivious to those cries, and the awesome truth is that He has done something – He has thrown us a line. On the wall of one of the churches in Cardiff that we use to host the Offensive Course, there's a banner that simply reads: *"Jesus God to the rescue."* I love it because in 5 words it sums up exactly what God has done to save the day – He sent His Son, Jesus (which literally means 'God Saves') to rescue us.

Jesus is the flesh and blood evidence that God's heart beats for lost people! Turning His back on the purity and bliss of heaven, Jesus put a skin-suit on and stepped right down to our level – straight into the middle of all the chaos. He was born in disgrace in a stinking shed next-door to a pub. He grew up in a rough neighbourhood, worked a common job, and had to eat, breathe, sleep and survive the same way as everyone else. Wherever He went He made an impression on people – some loved Him, others hated Him, but no one could ignore Him. Jesus, however, never lost sight of why He'd come:

*"For the Son of Man came to seek and to save the lost."* [5]

# 1. The Call.

One of the things that just knocks me out about Jesus is that rather than doing the whole 'saving the world' thing on His own, He chose instead to hand-pick a posse of dip-sticks to join Him on a life of adventure, mission and passionate sacrifice:

*"Passing alongside the Sea of Galilee, [Jesus] saw Simon and Andrew the brother of Simon casting a net into the sea, for they were fishermen. And Jesus said to them, 'Follow me and I will make you fishers of men.' And immediately they left their nets and followed Him."* [6]

# OFFENSIVE ☺

These 2 weren't the only ones to hear that call either. Fishermen, crooks, ruff-necks, prostitutes...you name it – they all ended up on Team Jesus! It's like my mate Andy Hawthorne once said: *"God's got no taste whatsoever – He'll use absolutely anybody!"*[7]

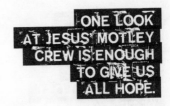

ONE LOOK AT JESUS' MOTLEY CREW IS ENOUGH TO GIVE US ALL HOPE.

I mean let's face it, if we got to pick God's rescue team for Him, we'd do it the classic school football team way – all the talented, popular superstars first, and all the rubbish, clueless misfits last!

The good news for us is that God doesn't work like that.

One look at Jesus' motley crew is enough to give us all hope. Sinful, selfish, doubting and denying – this lot were about as far removed from the Dream Team as you could possibly find. However, this was the team that Jesus wanted, so rather than sacking them, He stuck with them and led them on a mission that would ultimately change the face and future of the whole world.

That mission's still rolling on today, and Jesus wants us to be part of it!

## ADVENTURE

*"Follow me..."*

I was privileged enough to grow up in the 1980's when the A-Team, the Goonies and Indiana Jones ruled the screen! They might seem a bit old-school now, but back then they got the adrenaline of an entire generation pumping and were, without doubt, responsible for inspiring armies of kids (like me) to run round the streets with planks of wood, water-pistols and anything else we could find, to give whatever baddies we stumbled across a right pasting! Because of heroes like B.A Baracus I grew up hungry for adventure, longing to spend my time, energy and desires on something that inspired my dreams and excited my senses. (And if I got to save the universe in the process too – bonus!!!)

I bet you were the same.

Maybe you still are!

Either way, it's crucial that we understand that Jesus' call to follow Him is an invitation to so much more than the pointless and ultimately purposeless existence that life without God offers. It's a call to follow heaven's own Superhero on a life-changing journey of risk and radical faith.

**FOLLOWING JESUS WAS AND IS MEANT TO BE THE MOST LIBERATING, EXCITING LIFE YOU COULD EVER HOPE FOR!**

See I don't know about you, but I get kind of excited by the thought of hanging out with someone who walked on water, healed the sick, set people free from demons, embraced the poor, stuck up for the needy, wound-up religious hypocrites, smashed-up the tables of con-artists, turned water into wine, fed thousands with a packed-lunch, told storms to sit down and shut up and even raised the dead!

Following Jesus was and is meant to be the most liberating, exciting life you could ever hope for! God's got so much more in store for us than the pansy brand of Christianity that seems to be doing the rounds right now! Powerless, passionless, predictable and tame – it's little wonder that so few people want a piece of that! But we were never called to pursue the wet, weird and wimpy way of life that so many associate with following Jesus these days.

Stuff that!!!

I love how Erwin McManus puts it:

*"Jesus never made a pristine call to a proper or safe religion. Jesus beckons His followers to a path that is far from the easy road. It is a path filled with adventure, uncertainty, and unlimited possibilities – the only path that can fulfil the deepest longings and desires of your heart."* [8]

Jesus came to give us *"life in all its fullness."* [9] If we really want to live while we're alive, we need to be willing to obey Jesus' call to follow Him on the adventure of a life-time!

# OFFENSIVE ☉

## MISSION

*"…and I will make you fishers of men."*

When I was a squeaky little 12 year old I went to Newquay in Cornwall with my school rugby team. As you can imagine, most of us were well up for spending a week away from our parents, doing the whole beach, bedlam and boys on tour thing – but that's not why we were there. We were there to represent our school by thrashing a couple of local rugby teams (which we gladly did!) In the same way, following Jesus is about much more then going on tour with the Miracle Man, letting Him do all the graft while we get to party on the sidelines. Jesus didn't come to this world on holiday, He came to storm the gates of hell, rescue a shed-load of people, and invite a bunch of muppets (us lot) to roll our sleeves up and get in on the action too. Do you feel completely unqualified to answer that call? Me too! I mean who are we to be part of something as huge as this? Let's face it – I'm not a hero, and neither are you, but that's no excuse to just roll over and tap out. Besides it's not as if we're alone in our inadequacy…

When Jesus' disciples started out on the journey with Him, they were about as capable of reaching and rescuing the lost, as Homer Simpson is of walking past a Donut shop without dribbling! However, as they spent the next 3 years following Him, watching Him, learning from Him, making mistakes and yet experiencing His outrageous grace, they were gradually transformed into a new-breed of fishermen – not the sort that fished for salmon, but the sort that fished for souls! Did they fit the bill as heroes? Nope! Did they ever blow it? Yep! But they were still willing to answer the call, drop everything and follow Him – and that's all that Jesus required of them!

The truth is we'll never be more alive than when we're living out the adventure of mission with Jesus Christ.

## SACRIFICE

As we join Jesus on the most important search and rescue-mission in history, we do so knowing that saving others doesn't require

**CARRYING A CROSS AND DYING ON IT MIGHT SOUND A BIT INTENSE, BUT NO ONE HAS MORE RIGHT TO MAKE SUCH AN OUTRAGEOUS DEMAND THAN JESUS.**

charisma or skill, but commitment and sacrifice. Jesus put it like this:

*"If anyone would come after me, let Him deny himself, take up His cross and follow me. For whoever would save his life will lose it, but whoever loses his life for my sake and the gospel's will save it."* [10]

Death on a cross was one of the most barbaric ways of killing people ever invented and was very popular back in Jesus' day. Therefore, the graphic image of taking up a cross speaks of loving Jesus to death, and holding nothing back as we give all we've got to see His mission through to the end! Carrying a cross and dying on it might sound a bit intense, but no one has more right to make such an outrageous demand than Jesus. Remember that He Himself was a man on a mission – a cross-driven mission:

**AS WE ANSWER HIS CALL TO FOLLOW HIM, WE MUST DO SO KNOWING THAT IF HE WAS WILLING TO GO THE WAY OF THE CROSS – HE EXPECTS NOTHING LESS FROM US!**

*"The Son of Man came…to give His life as a ransom for many."* [11]

Incredibly, despite all the amazing miracles He performed, the lives He transformed and the mind-blowing words of wisdom that He spoke, the most inspirational and controversial Man to ever walk the earth was eventually betrayed, beaten-up and unjustly sentenced to a brutal death. He was forced to carry His own cross to a rubbish dump just outside Jerusalem City, where He was nailed to it and left to die. The physical pain He endured, however, was minimal compared to the spiritual agony that He suffered, as He soaked up the filth of the whole world and took the full weight of God's wrath for it all!

Not long before He breathed His last breath, Jesus cried out *"It is finished"*, declaring victoriously that His cross-driven mission was complete. What had looked like 'Mission Impossible' was now 'Mission Accomplished' and broken humanity at last had an escape-route!

Saving the world cost Jesus absolutely everything – He spilled His blood and sacrificed His very life so others may live. As we answer His call to follow Him, we must do so knowing that if He was willing to go the way of the cross – He expects nothing less from us!

# 2. The Command

The good news for the world, however, is that the cross wasn't the end – not for Jesus, and certainly not for us...

No doubt about it – the award for greatest come-back ever has got to go to Jesus! Pronounced dead at the scene, mummified to the max in grave-clothes, and sealed up in a tomb of solid rock for 3 days. Oh yeah, the SAS were on guard outside too – just in case any tomb-raiders showed up! But Jesus had promised loads of times that He'd beat the power of death and rise on the third day. And Jesus never breaks His promises!

So on day 3, when the earth shook, the angel ripped the stone away, and Jesus strolled out (past the petrified soldiers), you might have expected His boys to be waiting outside the tomb waving their 'Welcome Back' banners. (After all, it's not as if Jesus didn't have a successful track record in the miracle department!) But they were nowhere to be found. Where were they?

Hiding like turkeys at Christmas is where. Quaking in their boots. Gutted that their hero had died so brutally and so publicly, and worried that they'd be next! Jesus, however, remained committed to the rescue team that He'd spent so long putting together, so when He eventually tracked them down He told them straight that things were about to change in a big way. He told them that His work on earth was done, and that He was heading back to heaven, leaving them to finish what He had started.

In other words, it was time for the disciples to step up to the plate, and rather than simply tagging along on mission *with* Jesus, it was now time for them to step out on mission *for* Jesus.

This is how Jesus laid it out:

*"Go into all the world and preach the good news to everyone."* [12]

## GO EVERYWHERE

*"Go into all the world..."*

**THE CROSS-DRIVEN MISSION IS ALL ABOUT POPULATING HIS HEAVEN WITH PEOPLE THAT HE'S RESCUED FROM EVERY SINGLE PART OF OUR WORLD.**

The book of Revelation is without doubt one of the scariest, trippiest books in the whole Bible. At first glance, some of the stuff John (the bloke who wrote it) saw seems so freaked-out and trippy that you'd be forgiven for thinking that he was just some skunk-smoking hippy who dreamed the whole thing up during happy hour on the beach. However, a closer look makes you realise that what John saw was clearly inspired by God not induced by ganja! In fact, God blessed John with a brief glimpse of His future plans for this world and its people. One of the things that John experienced was the international flavour of heaven's worship anthem:

*"And they sang a new song with these words: 'You are worthy...For you were slaughtered, and your blood has ransomed people for God from every tribe and language and people and nation.'"* [13]

That just blows me away! Jesus wants us to know that the cross-driven mission is all about populating His heaven with people that He's rescued from every single part of our world. He wants us to know that no matter where people are at, what language they speak or what culture they're from – no one's beyond His reach because His blood has made it possible for them to take their place at His eternal praise party!

Now it's probably fair to say that back then Jesus' disciples didn't really have a clue how big the mission actually was, or how long it would take. A quick blast through the book of Acts, however, shows us that for a small crew they had a pretty good go! They literally did turn the known world upside down in a bid to make sure that all people everywhere would be touched by the awesome power of the gospel. Those first disciples are obviously long gone now, but the same mission still stands today, and 2000 years later, we've got a much better idea of just how big the job still is:

The world – a 7,926 mile round-trip across land and sea, ice and sand.

7 continents.

193 countries.

4,740 species of frog (totally irrelevant, but quite interesting!)

6.5 billion people (and still rising).

13,511(ish) languages.

And one Gospel!

Oh yeah – not everyone likes Jesus or Christians either!

Today, we can get pretty much anywhere in the world quicker than ever before. Satellite and web technology mean that we can write and talk to people in all sorts of random places, and even send pictures and videos across the world in seconds. To date, we've got more

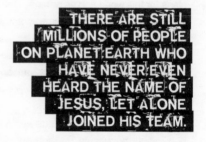

THERE ARE STILL MILLIONS OF PEOPLE ON PLANET EARTH WHO HAVE NEVER EVEN HEARD THE NAME OF JESUS, LET ALONE JOINED HIS TEAM.

Bibles in more languages, more missionaries in more countries, more money flowing through more mission agencies, more churches and more Christians than at any other point in history.

Not bad – but we're still not there!

The reality is that there are still millions of people on planet earth who have never even heard the name of Jesus, let alone joined His team. We need to realise that while many of these un-reached people are living in some of the most hardcore, anti-Jesus countries of the world – things are pretty bleak in our neck of the woods too! Stick the news on for 10 minutes if you need convincing!

**SITTING DOWN AND WARMING OUR BORN-AGAIN BUMS ON STONE-COLD CHURCH PEWS IS COMPLETELY MISSING THE POINT OF WHAT IT IS THAT JESUS HAS COMMANDED US TO DO.**

If we're going to effectively reach and rescue the lost people of our broken world, we need to accept that these days people just aren't queuing up outside our churches, desperate to come in for an encounter with the living God. In fact Jesus never said that they'd come to us at all. He told us to go to them – with their addictions, hurts, violence, hang-ups, curses, fears, promiscuity, doubts, bitterness, brokenness, and deep, deep need.

He told us to go to people just like we were before God's grace caught up with us!!!

Whether it means crossing continents and cultures, or simply crossing the street – our world needs Jesus as much as it ever did, and we're the ones He's trusted to go and introduce them to Him! Sitting down and warming our born-again bums on stone-cold church pews as we wait for desperate and dying people to come to us for help, is completely missing the point of what it is that Jesus has commanded us to do.

He's told us to go!

## PLUNGE

When I was a head-shot teenager I went up to North Wales with some mates and we went to this beautiful little Snowdonian town called Betws-y-Coed. In the middle of the town is a bridge over a fast-flowing waterfall about 30ft below. The boys I was with decided that it was a good idea to jump off the bridge into the river...so they did!

Nutters!!!

So there I was, the only one left standing on the edge of the bridge like Billy No-Mates, knowing that if I didn't jump I'd regret it forever. The thing is it looked

like a proper laugh and I really wanted to do it – but I wasn't just scared – I was producing bricks at a rate of knots!!! However, in the end fear gave way to stupidity and I closed my eyes and just launched myself...

It felt like I was in mid-air for hours and I'd already run out of breath before I eventually hit the water – SPLAAADOOOOOOOSSSH!!!

When I eventually re-surfaced, the adrenaline was pumping through my body faster than Sonic the Hedgehog on Red Bull, but I was so stoked that I went straight back up and did it all

> **JESUS HAS TOLD US TO GO, AND THAT'S GOING TO TAKE GUTS AND OBEDIENCE!**

again! Despite the fact that I was rushed to hospital two days later (throwing up blood) I was just glad that I'd conquered my fear and done it!

See, the thing with fear is that it can stop us from doing and achieving so much. It cripples us! For Christians, this is never more real than when it comes to stepping out on the cross-driven mission! Jesus has told us to GO, and that's going to take Guts and Obedience! He never promised that the mission would be easy. As we've seen, saving people is often costly, and painful (as the cross should always remind us), but for the sake of the lost, we need to reach beyond our fear, take the plunge and just go for it!

## TELL EVERYONE

*"preach the good news to everyone."*

In the final moments of Peter Jackson's epic film adaptation of Tolkien's Lord Of The Rings trilogy, after almost 9 hours of Ring-bearing, Orc-slaying, Middle-Earth mayhem, it all gets a bit hectic when Frodo and Gollum start swinging handbags at each other in the middle of Mount Doom. They both end up falling off a cliff, and as Gollum gets deep-fried with the 'precious' in a lake of molten lava, Frodo (minus one of his fingers) is left hanging precariously over the burning cauldron below. Fortunately for Frodo, his best-mate Sam is on hand to save his skin. Sam, as he reaches over the edge of the cliff, urges Frodo: *"Give me your hand. Take my hand. Don't you let go. Don't let go...Reach!"*

It's an amazing picture of what the cross-driven mission is all about – not just reaching out to the lost, but urging them to reach out and grab hold of the only one who can rescue them – Jesus. It's important we understand that once we've stepped to where people are at, we've also then got to find the courage to open our mouths and tell them what they need to hear if they want to reach safety. This is called preaching.

The Greek word for 'preach' used here is 'kerusso' which is a strong word for declaring something that's of such immense importance that it demands a response! In other words, we're not called to go into all the world to merely share some fluffy five-minute thought for the day, make a couple of lifestyle suggestions, or offer yet another 'perspective' to the ongoing debate about the meaning of life. True preaching means telling people the truth about themselves and God, and urging them from depths of our guts, to turn to Him and trust His gospel to save them! The Greek word for 'gospel' is 'euaggelion' (where we get the word evangelism from) and it literally means 'to preach good news!' In other words, the good news is that we get to preach a message of such good news that it's just got to be preached!

**IF WE WANT TO SEE THE PEOPLE AROUND US SAVED – WE NEED TO UNLOCK OUR LIPS AND TELL THEM ABOUT THE ONLY ONE WHO CAN DO IT!**

There's a lot more to preaching than simply screaming at people on the High Street, or thumping a sturdy oak pulpit on a Sunday. There are plenty of other ways that we can tell people about Jesus too: over a cappuccino in Starbucks (coffeevangelism), chatting to someone on the bus (double-deckervangelism), even online (wwwdottyvangelism)! Some of the most amazing opportunities that I've ever had to tell people about Jesus have been when I'm out on the streets walking my dog in the middle of the night (doggyvangelism)!

The next chapter goes much deeper into exactly what our rescue-message is, but in short, if we want to see the people around us saved – we need to unlock our lips and tell them about the only One who can do it!

# OFFENSIVE ◑

## HIT-AND-RUN

Now while we're on the subject of preaching the gospel, it's worth mentioning that Jesus was never into smashing people over the head with a hefty, leather-bound über-Bible, getting them to 'pray the prayer' then leaving them

> LET'S BE ABOUT BUILDING AN ARMY OF DISCIPLES WHO ARE SO PROUD OF THE NAME OF JESUS THAT THEY PUT US TO SHAME AS THEY TAKE THEIR PASSION TO THE STREETS.

dazed and confused in a heap, wondering what had just hit them. That's hit-and-run evangelism and despite what some might think – it's not what Jesus was about.

Jesus was all about making disciples and He's told us to do the same.[14]

The Greek word for 'making disciples' in the Bible simply means to 'teach' or to 'instruct' and it speaks of establishing life-long commitments, not short-term, superficial decisions. Keith Green once wrote that *"God would rather see one true convert than an ocean full of 'decisions.'"*[15] Therefore, as we go about the business of preaching the gospel to our generation, let's be serious about seeking and reaching the lost, but just as serious about keeping and teaching them too! Let's remember that when the gospel takes root in someone's life it's the start of the journey, not the end of the road. Let's not settle for closet conversions that might give us a little ego-trip, but do nothing to change the world. Rather, let's be about building an army of disciples who are so proud of the Name of Jesus that they put us to shame as they take their passion to the streets.

## GIVE EVERYTHING

In the first chapter of the Book of Acts (God's "How To Start Your Church With A Bang" Manual) we catch up with the disciples receiving their final orders from Jesus just before He goes back to Heaven. He tells them to get ready for some Holy Spirit fire-works, and then encourages

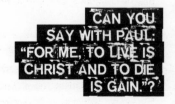

> CAN YOU SAY WITH PAUL: "FOR ME, TO LIVE IS CHRIST AND TO DIE IS GAIN."?

them with these words: *"you will be my witnesses, telling people about me everywhere – in Jerusalem, throughout Judea, in Samaria, and to the ends of the earth."* [16]

The Greek word for 'witnesses' is 'martus' which is where we get the word 'martyrs' from. In other words, Jesus was telling His boys that the cross-driven mission was going to transform the entire world, but would cost them everything – even their own lives! Incredibly, out of those 11 disciples – 10 died as martyrs!

I love the story of James Calvert who, back in the nineteenth century, went on a mission to introduce the cannibals of the Fiji Islands to Jesus. The captain of the ship he was sailing on pleaded with him not to go, saying: *"You will lose your life and the lives of those with you if you go among such savages."* Calvert's reply was awesome: *"We died before we came here."*

Is that where you are at? Are you willing to go anywhere and give everything for the sake of the lost? Is anything more important to you than playing your part in the cross-driven mission? Does your own comfort and even your own life come second to your commitment to seeing 'savages' saved and set free? Have you been *"crucified with Christ"* [17] and died to all selfishness, worldliness and fear? Is Jesus Christ and His rescue-mission really what you're living for? Can you say with Paul: *"For me, to live is Christ and to die is gain."*? [18]

In 1956 a young American missionary called Jim Elliot was murdered by the Aucas – a tribe of Indians in Ecuador that he was passionate about reaching with the Gospel. Decades later, he is still remembered for these powerful words: *"He is no fool who gives up what he cannot keep to gain that which he cannot lose."* [19] Elliot knew that the only thing worth giving his life for was the only thing that he could take with him when he died – souls saved by Jesus!

Right in front of us there's a world that needs saving, and whether it's our mates in school or work, the gangs on street-corners, or the hardest, darkest, Jesus-hating places of the world, we need to be obedient, to count the cost and go. We might not all end up on the international front-line dodging bullets for Jesus. For many of us our part of the mission will involve reaching out locally in schools, skateparks, sports centres, salons, supermarkets, even our own streets and sofas, whilst praying for and financially supporting those who have been called to graft away in other parts of the world. However, as George Whitfield once said *"We must all have the spirit of martyrdom, though we may not all die martyrs."*[20]

Jesus isn't looking for super-saints who've got a lot to give. What He's looking for is an army of selfless soldiers who are willing to give Him everything they've got.

## SCOOBY VS SCRAPPY

"Go."

It's the shortest command in the whole Bible, but without doubt it's also one of the biggest! Two little letters. Two possible responses: Scooby Doo or Scrappy Doo! Which one are you?

> **GOD IS LOOKING FOR SCRAPPY DOO'S WHO'LL GO ANYWHERE AND DO ANYTHING FOR HIM, NO MATTER WHAT THE COST!**

Scooby Doo's the human-size dog who gets most of the fame and attention, but he's actually just a big coward who's more into stuffing his face than solving mysteries. Scooby's the one who's always running away from danger crying like a baby! His little nephew Scrappy Doo, on the other hand, is the total opposite – a powerful little package of pumped-up puppy who's up for anything, fears nothing and never knows when to give up! He's the one who the others have to drag away from danger, still swinging punches and shouting *"Lemme at 'em! Lemme at 'em!!!"*

When it comes to the cross-driven mission, Scooby Doo saints just don't cut it. God is looking for Scrappy Doo's who'll go anywhere and do anything for Him, no matter what the cost! Unfortunately, however, there are many Christian Scooby's who are happy to do the whole church thing, but who genuinely believe that mission isn't for them, that it's not their thing or that God hasn't called them to go. But that is categorically not what Jesus or the Bible teach, as William Booth (the bloke who set-up the Salvation Army) made quite clear:

*"'Not called!' did you say? 'Not heard the call,' I think you should say. Put your ear down to the Bible, and hear Him bid you go and pull sinners out of the fire of sin. Put your ear down to the burdened, agonized heart of humanity, and listen to its pitiful wail for help. Go stand by the gates of hell, and hear the damned entreat you to go to their father's house and bid their brothers and sisters and servants and masters not to come there. Then look Christ in the face – whose mercy you have professed to obey – and tell Him whether you will join heart and soul and body and circumstances in the march to publish His mercy to the world."*

Now that might sound a bit full-on, but it comes from a deep awareness that all Christians are called to be life-saving, cross-driven missionaries, whoever and wherever they are! That includes you. Jesus didn't die for us in order that we could just get fat and lazy as we sit twiddling our thumbs waiting for the bus to heaven. We were saved for service, as Erwin McManus also said: *"Salvation is not re-entry into a Paradise Lost; it's enlistment in the mission of God."* [21]

If you're a Christian you're part of the mission – it's as simple as that. The truth is that whether we like it or not, we're living slap-bang in the middle of a war-zone, though the battle's not against people, it's for people. It's not a jihad or holy war – it's the good fight of faith, and we don't carry hand-grenades or AK-47's, we carry a cross. The cross-driven mission is essentially a search and rescue adventure that we are privileged to be part of.

**THERE'S NO ONE MORE CALLED OR BETTER PLACED TO REACH THE PEOPLE IN YOUR BIT OF THE WORLD THAN YOU!**

However, another thing that can squash the Scrappy Doo out of us and stop us 'going' for Jesus isn't so much that we don't feel called, but rather that we don't feel ready – that it's just not the right time.

*"I'll wait til I'm older."*

*"I've got to sort this other stuff in my life out first."*

*"I need more guidance."*

*"I'll go once I'm married, once I'm qualified, once I'm needed..."*

## OFFENSIVE ⟳

The thing is, none of these are good enough excuses to stop us going because people need saving all around us right now! We need to take responsibility for our generation. If we don't then who will? There's no one more called or better placed to reach the people in your bit of the world than you! So what are you going to do about it?

AS THE WORLD AROUND US CONTINUES TO SLIP AND SLIDE INTO OBLIVION, WE NEED TO TAKE THE INITIATIVE, GO ON THE OFFENSIVE AND SAVE AS MANY AS WE CAN!

It's crucial that we realise that this isn't like Mission Impossible, where Tom Cruise gets given the option of *"Your mission, should you choose to accept it…"* (Just before the message blows up!) This mission isn't a mere suggestion. It's a call to action that comes direct from Jesus Himself! Therefore, as the world around us continues to slip and slide into oblivion, we need to take the initiative, go on the offensive and save as many as we can!

## 3. The Comfort

Anyone who thinks that following Jesus is going to be safe has clearly never tried it properly (or read the New Testament!) I've lost track of all the jokes, the sniping comments, the strange looks and people thinking I'm nuts. Not to mention all the times I've had my heart broken as people have thrown grace back in my face! I've had someone threaten to come and stab me up when they got out of jail. I've had property damaged, my flat robbed and my youth club smashed-up. I even had a kebab posted through my letter-box once (but I wasn't sure if that was persecution of provision!)

And don't get me wrong – I've got nothing on the Apostle Paul…

*"I have worked harder, been put in jail more often, been whipped times without number, and faced death again and again. Five different times the Jews gave me the thirty-nine lashes. Three times I was beaten with rods. Once I was stoned. Three times I was shipwrecked. Once I spent a whole night and a day adrift at*

*sea. I have travelled many weary miles. I have faced danger from flooded rivers and from robbers. I have faced danger from my own people, the Jews, as well as from the Gentiles. I have faced danger in the cities, in the deserts, and on the stormy seas. And I have faced danger from men who claim to be Christians but are not. I have lived with weariness and pain and sleepless nights. Often I have been hungry and thirsty and have gone without food. Often I have shivered with cold without enough clothing to keep me warm."* [22]

How on earth do you keep going through stuff like that? What do you do when the rubber really hits the road and people start treating us like scum, all in the name of the cross-driven mission?

We simply need to take Jesus at His word when He said: *"I am with you always, even to the end of the age."* [23]

This is a real promise that comes from the lips of the real God.

On the same wall of that church I was on about is another banner that says: "Immanuel God With Us." That was another one of Jesus' titles. He didn't just come to save us – He came to be with us. Permanently!

Jesus is with us.

He wants to be us.

He wants to be with us so bad that He died to make it happen!

I don't know about you, but I find that incredibly comforting!

## EN-COURAGE

I love that Jesus didn't just boot His boys out of the door with a 'come back when you've finished' attitude while He put His feet up and puffed on a cigar. The cross-driven mission is *His mission*, and He's more committed to getting it done than anyone! His heart is to save people – it always has been, so it's little wonder that He's committed to staying right by our side as we walk the mission field of the world. He might have now left us physically, but He still walks alongside us, by the power of the Holy Spirit, ready to pour His mercy out through us and into the lives of the people around us. So as we seek out the lost to

**THERE'S NOTHING AND NO ONE THAT CAN STAND AGAINST HIM, SO THERE'S NOTHING AND NO ONE THAT CAN STAND AGAINST US.**

help them find safety and security in Jesus, we go with the knowledge that there's nothing and no one that can stand against Him, so there's nothing and no one that can stand against us. Sure, sometimes it really can feel like the whole world is against us, but because we've got the hero of heaven on our side, we can look any enemy, problem or situation in the eye and say *"If you think you're hard – check out my mate!"*

The word 'encourage' literally means to 'give courage to...' and that's precisely what Jesus wants us to get from His promise to be permanently present with us.

We go with courageous hearts because He'll never leave or forsake us.[24]

We go with happy hearts because in His presence is fullness of joy.[25]

And we go with strong hearts because the joy of the LORD is our strength![26]

As we step out on the cross-driven mission, we go with Jesus before us saying *"Follow me on the wildest adventure you'll ever have!"* We go with Jesus behind us saying: *"Go for it, and change the world in my name!"* And we go with Jesus right by our side saying: *"I'm with you all the way!"*

# THE AFTERMATH

# BEN'S STORY

" I was first involved with the Offensive course back in 2006. I'd been going to church all my life and so the message of the Gospel was nothing new to me. Although I didn't realise it, even as a Christian I'd probably heard so many people talking about Jesus I was bored of it and it often went in one ear and out the other.

Offensive helped me realise that actually God sending his Son to die for me is the most incredible, and undeserved gift I can ever receive. It's amazing! I became astounded at how great the price was that Jesus paid to allow me to have a never-ending relationship with God, and yet totally humbled at the foot of the cross.

Once I grasped a little bit of the immensity of God's grace for me, there could only be one response, and that was to share it with others. At 16 I was full of selfish dreams and prideful ambition. I had my life planned out, to be successful, rich and sorted. However the world doesn't need more Christians like that. It needs Christians that are ready to waste their lives on proclaiming the gospel, and demonstrating God's grace through the church.

What an awesome adventure, I can't think of anything I'd rather be a part of no matter what it might cost... "

# CHAPTER TWO

## SHOUT OUT!

"WOE TO ME IF I DO NOT PREACH THE GOSPEL!"[27]

**- APOSTLE PAUL**

# OFFENSIVE 🔥

## SWEET FEET

*My feet are minging!*

I'm not kidding. Following a catalogue of nasty skateboarding injuries and subsequent operations, my scarred feet are so mangled and messed-up that one look is enough to make most surgeons

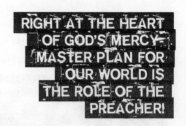

RIGHT AT THE HEART OF GOD'S MERCY-MASTER PLAN FOR OUR WORLD IS THE ROLE OF THE PREACHER!

shudder and small children cry! I've had a permanent limp since I was about 20 and although some people think I'm just trying to strut like a gangster with a gunshot wound, it's purely just that I've got some majorly mashed-up flippers!

Which is why I love the bit in the Bible that says that my feet are actually beautiful – and so are yours!

Seriously, take off your shoes and socks and have a good hard look at your digits! OK, before you think I'm a total nut-bar, I'd better explain what I'm going on about. God's given us an incredible rescue message for our lost world: *"everyone who calls on the name of the Lord will be saved."* [28] But with that awesome truth comes a massive responsibility:

*"How then will they call on him in whom they have not believed? And how are they to believe in him of whom they have never heard? And how are they to hear without someone preaching? And how are they to preach unless they are sent? As it is written, "How beautiful are the feet of those who preach the good news!"* [29]

Right at the heart of God's mercy-master plan for our world is the role of the preacher! Yes Jesus is the only One who can save humanity, but how are people going to turn to Him if they've never even heard about Him? And how are they going to hear unless someone's got the grace and guts to take a few risks and tell them? The reality is that more than anything else, this world needs people with 'beautiful feet', who are willing to boldly go where no man's gone before and point people to Jesus.

The world needs preachers.

# SHOUT OUT!

Without doubt the sweetest feet to ever grace this planet are the ones that belong to Jesus Himself. He sent sickness packing, gave demons a kicking, and even put the smack-down on death itself. But first and foremost Jesus was a preacher. Check out how He launched His gospel adventure: *"Jesus came into Galilee, proclaiming the gospel of God."* [30]

**GOD HAS BLESSED US WITH A BEAUTIFUL, LIFE-CHANGING MESSAGE THAT'S WORTH SHOUTING OUR HEADS OFF ABOUT.**

Remember that gospel simply means good news, and Jesus' 'beautiful feet' took Him on a gospel tour-de-force that didn't stop until they were eventually nailed to a Roman cross – and even then it wasn't all over. Jesus was still preaching the gospel as He died, still preaching it after He'd beaten death, and then, just before heading home to heaven, He handed us the baton and told us to complete the mission and carry on preaching the same gospel! The good news is that the gospel is still good news for a bad news world that's absolutely gagging for some good news! God has blessed us with a beautiful, life-changing message that's worth shouting our heads off about.

OK, my prayer is that two things will happen as you get stuck into this chapter. Firstly, that you get completely and utterly overwhelmed by a fresh understanding of the immensity of God's grace that He saved you at all, let alone made you part of His team to save humanity! And secondly that an irresistible sense of urgency, expectation, courage and faith starts rising up inside your guts as God impresses on you that actually – this gospel works, and is all you need to change the world in His name.

So what exactly is the Gospel?

New Testament heavyweight preacher Paul (a one-time Jesus-hating terrorist who God transformed into a world-changing evangelist) once defined the Gospel for us in a single simple sentence:

*"Now I would remind you, brothers, of the gospel I preached to you...that Christ died for our sins in accordance with the scriptures, that he was buried, that he was raised on the third day according to the scriptures, and that he appeared to ..."* [31]

That's our message in a nut-shell: Jesus died for our sins, got buried and rose again on day three, (just like the Bible says) and He's still in the business of showing up in people's lives today! The Gospel revolves around the person of Jesus, His death on the cross and His incredible resurrection.

# 1. The Christ

The Gospel of Mark opens with these words: *"The beginning of the Gospel of Jesus Christ, the Son of God."* [32] In other words it's Jesus' gospel. His story. He's the real hero – the One who saves the day. For those of us who've chosen the path of the cross-driven mission there's only one name that should be on our lips – and that's the name of Jesus. Why? Because *"Salvation is found in no one else, for there is no other name under heaven given to men by which we must be saved."* [33]

Jim Elliot once said, *"Missionaries are very human folks, just doing what they are asked. Simply a bunch of nobodies trying to exalt somebody."* [34]

That 'somebody' is Jesus Christ!

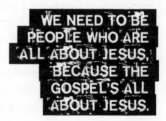

WE NEED TO BE PEOPLE WHO ARE ALL ABOUT JESUS, BECAUSE THE GOSPEL'S ALL ABOUT JESUS.

We need to be people who are all about Jesus, because the Gospel's all about Jesus. However, it's not just who Jesus is that we're to shout about. We need to unzip our lips about what He's done too.

At the core of the cross-driven mission is the message of the cross of Jesus.

# 2. The Cross

*"Christ died for our sins..."*

It's inspired more films, more books and more art than anything else ever. It's become so 'cool' that we now see it tattooed on people's skin, fashioned into jewellery and hanging round the necks of all sorts of people from grandmothers to gangsta rappers.

It's now such a common symbol that it's easy to forget that the cross is one of the most brutal ways of killing people ever devised!

**JESUS' CRUCIFIXION IS THE MOST MONUMENTAL, LIFE-CHANGING, WORLD-SHAPING EVENT IN HUMAN HISTORY,** Without going into too much graphic detail, those who were sentenced to be crucified were normally stripped and beaten-up, before being forced to carry a huge cross-beam of wood to the place where they would die. Their arms were stretched out and crude nails were hammered into each hand to pin them to the cross-beam. They were then hoisted up onto a tree or a vertical mast and a spike was driven through both feet. People walking past would laugh, spit and insult them as they battled for the next breath. It could take days to die. Dying on a cross was humiliating and excruciatingly painful, and was described by Jewish historian Josephus as *"the most wretched of deaths."* [35]

Incredibly, however, it was the way that God chose to save the world. Jesus' crucifixion is the most monumental, life-changing, world-shaping event in human history, yet is recorded in the Bible with just 3 simple words, **"they crucified Him."** [36]

The entire Old Testament pointed to the cross. Jesus' whole ministry pointed to the cross. And everywhere that the New Testament missionaries went, they pointed people to the cross of Jesus.

Why?

# OFFENSIVE ⟳

If we really want to get to understand why the cross is such good news, we need to understand exactly why He had to die.

Christ died for our sins.

## SIN

Sin is not a popular word these days, and not many people know either what it is or how serious it actually is. Simply defined, sin is rebelling against God. Ever since Adam and Eve ate the forbidden fruit in Genesis chapter 3, the virus of sin has been spreading across the planet, infecting every single person who's ever lived:

SIN IS BEHIND EVERYTHING IN OUR WORLD THAT'S EVIL AND TWISTED AND WRONG

*"For all have sinned and fall short of the glory of God."* [37]

Sin is behind everything in our world that's evil and twisted and wrong. From the really obvious stuff like terrorism, murder, rape and theft, to the more subtle stuff like pride, jealousy, anger and hatred (and everything in between), sin contaminates the very fabric of who we are and affects the things we do, say and think. Sin is deeply offensive to God (who's perfect) and as a result it separates us from Him, both in this life, and after we die, in hell:

*"For the wages of sin is death"* [38]

Jesus talked more about hell than He did about heaven, but people don't like the idea of hell – they find it offensive. The trouble is that whether we choose to believe in something or not doesn't alter whether it's true or not! For example if you jumped out of a plane without a parachute, it makes no difference whether you choose to believe in gravity.

*SPLAT!!!*

> *Gravity's real!*
> > *Hell is real!*

JESUS CAME TO SAVE PEOPLE FROM THE ETERNAL TRAGEDY THAT THEY'RE HEADING FOR AND OUR PREACHING SHOULD REFLECT THAT.

However, we need to remember that: *"God did not send His Son into the world to condemn it, but to save it."*[39] To make a relationship between a perfect God and messed-up people like us possible. Yes, it is a fearful thing to fall into the hands of the living God, but let's not forget that those same hands bear the mercy marks of the cross. Jesus came to save people from the eternal tragedy that they're heading for and our preaching should reflect that.

## SNAP!

Back in 2001 I was cruising around Cardiff Skatepark, when it all went horribly wrong…

It was a trick I'd landed shed-loads of times before – dropping in down a steep flat-bank, busting a chunky pop-shuvit over the fun-box and rolling away shmoooove like chocolate down the other side. Only on this particular occasion I didn't roll away!

*Snap!!!*

You know you're in trouble when you don't just feel something break inside your knee – you audibly hear it too!

It wasn't the first time I'd busted myself up skateboarding, as my dislocated elbow, broken finger, arthritis, repeatedly broken ankles and permanently numb left buttock would readily testify, but I knew that this time it was super-bad. After being rushed to hospital in an ambulance I was reliably informed by an über-qualified medical professional that there was nothing seriously wrong with me and that I'd feel better in the morning.

As I hobbled out of A&E on a token pair of crutches, however, I wasn't convinced…

After a night of agony and very little sleep, I went back to hospital the following morning to see if there was anyone there who would believe that my leg was as mashed-up as it felt (or at least give me some morphine!) Praise God there was a knee specialist there, who plonked me down, sat on my foot and proceeded to pull my shin about like she was in the tug of war world cup. The fact that she could pretty much pull my lower leg an inch out of my knee-cap was all the evidence she needed: *"I'm afraid you've ruptured you ACL"*, she said, which was a technical way of saying that I'd ripped my cruciate ligament clean in half (a diagnosis that was later confirmed by a scan). OK – the bad news was that it was a very serious injury and in my current state I'd never be able to skate or do sport ever again.

However, the good news was that there was an operation they could do that would fix the problem and get things back to how they should be. A year later they knocked me out, cut my leg open like a piece of cheese, tweaked, twisted, stretched and stapled a few bits and bobs, and my knee's been sorted ever since.

I share that story because the first doctor did me no favours by giving me the 'good news' that I was fine, when actually my knee was completely mullered! The second doctor brought me face to face with the reality of my broken situation then pointed me to the surgeon who could sort me out. As people all around us are getting trashed by sin and its effects in their lives, they don't need someone to just make them feel better. Rather they need someone to make them really better. To take away their sin, heal their pain and give them their lives back.

The only one who can do that is Jesus.

The world is sick and the cross is the cure, but we can't expect people to embrace it if we don't tell them what the problem is! We need to have the guts to help people see how bad the bad news really is, so that they will see the gospel of Jesus as God's incredible good news for them. Unfortunately, too many people preach about sin and hell with such cold-blooded, loveless, arrogance that it does nothing to attract lost people to Jesus, but rather alienates them and turns them away from the gospel all together.

As we plead with people to trust Jesus to save them from sin, death and hell, we must do so with compassion in our hearts and tears in our eyes.

## MERCY

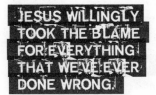

JESUS WILLINGLY TOOK THE BLAME FOR EVERYTHING THAT WE'VE EVER DONE WRONG.

OK, tough part over. Now strap yourself in and brace yourself for blessing as we remember exactly why the cross is such good news. Check out what was actually happening as Jesus died...

*"God made Him who had no sin to be sin for us..."* [40]

On the cross, Jesus, the perfect Son of God, literally became sin for us! That's just gob-smacking! Jesus willingly took the blame for everything that we've ever done wrong. He took the guilt for all our sin (every last bit of it), and all the other messed-up, filthy, evil stuff that people do. You name it – Christ became it!

Why?

Because God's all about perfect justice so He *must* punish sin. But His cross also proves that He's also all about outrageous mercy: He'd rather let the Son that He loves face the full weight of His judgement, than see the people He loves (us!) pay for it ourselves in hell! It's not that we were never guilty – far from it! It's that Jesus took our place, our blame and our punishment! That's why as Jesus hung on the cross He gasped *"My God, my God, why have You forsaken me?"* [41]

The answer to that question is "_____" (Your name!!!)

Jesus was forsaken (which means 'rejected') instead of you.

He died in your place. Sin was punished. Justice was done.

He took hell so that you'll never have to.

# OFFENSIVE

Mercy was once described as God not giving us what we deserve! It's true! That's why one of the songwriters in the Bible once wrote *"Praise the LORD, O my soul…He does not treat us as our sins deserve."* [42]

How much does our world need a piece of that?!

## GRACE

But it gets even better than that! As well as the outrageous mercy that we find at the cross, we also find something else that's so revolutionary it's going to change the world – the amazing grace of God! Grace is one of the most radical, world-shaking, lovingly-genius gifts that God has given us!

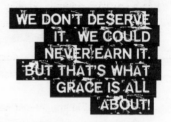

WE DON'T DESERVE IT. WE COULD NEVER EARN IT. BUT THAT'S WHAT GRACE IS ALL ABOUT!

If mercy's not getting what we *do* deserve, then grace can only be described as God giving us what we totally *don't* deserve! We don't just avoid hell (which is a miracle in itself!) but because of what Jesus did for us, we get so much more than that:

*"God made Him who had no sin to be sin for us, so that in Him we might become the righteousness of God."*

At the cross we can actually *become* God's righteousness! It sounds a bit crazy, so try to think of it as Jesus taking our filthy rags away and kitting us out in the freshest clothes there are – clothes fit for heaven! No more blame. No more shame. Just Jesus' purity and perfection credited to us! We don't deserve it. We could never earn it. But that's what grace is all about!

One of the most incredible pictures of grace is seen as Jesus was crucified between two thieves. All three of them would be dead in a few hours. One thief died cursing Jesus, while the other admitted his guilt and turned to Him for grace.

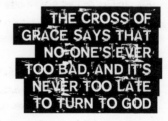

THE CROSS OF GRACE SAYS THAT NO-ONE'S EVER TOO BAD, AND IT'S NEVER TOO LATE TO TURN TO GOD

And grace is what he got:

*"Then [the thief] said, 'Jesus, remember me when you come into your kingdom'. Jesus answered him, 'I tell you the truth, today you will be with me in paradise.'"*[43]

He didn't have time to fix his life or prove that he'd changed – all he could do was hang there and die. However, death wasn't something for him to fear anymore, because he had Jesus' word that as he breathed out his last breath as a crucified criminal, his very next breath would be the fresh-air of heaven – the ultimate gangster's paradise!

The cross of grace says that no-one's ever too bad, and it's never too late to turn to God and grab hold of His promise of paradise!

That's the kind of gospel that people all around us are gagging for!!!

That's a message worth shouting about!

## FORGIVENESS

Have you ever done something so wrong that you just can't get away from the memory of it? No matter where you turn or what you do – you just feel dirty on the inside, and there's no soap or substance that can scrub you clean.

I have.

By the time is was 15 years old, I had done so much bad stuff that I lived with constant regret and self-hatred hanging over me! It was like I just couldn't get away from the memory of it all? No matter where I went, who I was with, or what I did (or drunk) – I just always felt dirty on the inside, and like my shadow, I just couldn't shake it off!

That's called guilt, and when guilt gets a grip – it doesn't let go! Guilt destroys people! It can drive them to drug addiction, alcoholism, self-harm and violence. It wrecks marriages, families and even communities, and it robs people of happiness and hope. Doctors and psychologists will tell you that if many of their patients were free of guilt, the demand for all the anti-depressants that they dish out would pretty much disappear overnight!

The truth is we all need forgiveness.

We're desperate for it!

Jesus' dying prayer for us on the cross was *"Father, forgive them, for they don't know what they are doing."*[44] He was praying for the people who were crucifying Him, but seeing as it was our sin that He was dying for – that makes us just as guilty as the Roman soldier that was smashing nails into His hands and feet!

God's heart for this world that He loves is forgiveness. It always was.

Centuries earlier, there was a famous King in the Bible called David who was no stranger to guilt. Amongst other stuff, he'd bedded another man's wife, got her pregnant and then arranged for her husband to be killed. When he finally ran out of places to run and faced up to God, he said something shocking:

*"Against You, and You alone, have I sinned;"* [45]

Ugh?! He's slept with someone else's wife (adultery) and arranged her husband's death (murder)! Hasn't he sinned against them too? How's it only God that he's offended?

It sounds scandalous, but we need to get our heads around this in order to fully understand the power of the cross. See, if you do something wrong against someone else, then the done thing is to ask them to forgive you. If they do – great!

But what if they don't?

What if they refuse to ever forgive you? (We all know what that feels like!)

The only options left are guilt or anger (both of which destroy you!) and that's where a lot of people are at right now!

However, if we see that all our sin is first and foremost offensive to God, and that when we do wrong stuff to others, it's actually God's perfect law that we're

> YOU KIND OF GET THE IDEA THAT WHEN GOD FORGIVES US – WE'RE NEVER GOING TO HAVE TO FACE OUR SIN AGAIN!

breaking – it changes our focus so that first-up we need to ask God for His forgiveness.

And God loves to forgive people.

That's why David could later write:

*"He has removed our sins from us as far as the east is from the west."* [46]

In a universe that's billions and billions of light years wide in each direction (and still counting!) You kind of get the idea that when God forgives us – we're never going to have to face our sin again!

That's forgiveness God-style!

When I was 15 I stopped running from God when I realised that Jesus' cross was for me! With tears in my eyes I handed my life over to Him and asked Him to forgive me for everything. There and then I felt the weight of fifteen years of just lifted off my shoulders, and for the first time ever I felt clean on the inside. I haven't been able to stop shouting about it ever since!

However, it wasn't until much later that I really got to grips with just how God's forgiveness works...

## BLOOD

You can't go through a daytime TV commercial break without at least one washing powder advert claiming to be able to wash things 'whiter than white!' Well that's fine for pants and plates but what about the human soul? Is there a way for us get all the dirt washed out of our lives?

Yes! Here it is...

Back in the Old Testament people could only get God's forgiveness by spilling the blood of a sacrificed animal (often a lamb). We might not fully understand how or why it works, but the Bible's clear: *"without the shedding of blood there is no forgiveness."* [47] When Jesus died on the cross, He was God's perfect Lamb that was sacrificed for us. That's why everyone who turns to Jesus and is *"washed in His blood"* can now experience His forgiveness. The good news message that we're running

> THE CHAINS OF SLAVERY HAVE BEEN SNAPPED TO BITS, AND WE CAN KNOW THE REALITY OF TRUE SPIRITUAL LIBERTY AND FREEDOM FROM THE SOUL-DESTROYING, LIFE-TRASHING EFFECTS OF SIN.

with is that the blood of Jesus DOES wash souls whiter than white! We need to be shouting our heads off about Jesus, His cross and His blood because *"the blood of Jesus, [God's] Son, cleanses us from all sin."* [48]

Charles Wesley wrote in one of his songs back in the 18th century:

*"His blood can make the foulest clean."* [49]

That's a message worth shouting about!

### FREEDOM

In the early hours of 3rd July 2007, BBC journalist Alan Johnson was released after being held as a hostage for 16 weeks by Islamic terrorists in Palestine. Clearly relieved upon his release, he said: *"You have to have been a prisoner to know how good freedom is."* [50] I love that statement, because for those of us who've encountered Jesus and set out on His cross-driven mission – that's our story and that's our message!

Jesus' blood washes us clean which is fantastic, but there's even more to the blood-message than that! *"[Jesus] came...to give his life as a ransom for many."* [51]

Back in Eden's Garden Adam and Eve basically sold the whole human race into slavery. Since that first act of rebellion against God, every one of us is now born in the grip of sin's chains and all of its consequences. The tragedy is that we weren't designed to be sin's slaves but God's kids, but it's impossible to deny the reality of our chains as we daily battle against bad habits, addictions, negative attitudes, pride. The only way for us to be set free and to enjoy being part of God's family is for someone to pay our ransom. We can't afford to pay because it costs the ultimate price – a perfect life (something none of us have got!) So Jesus stepped-up to make that payment on the cross and buy us back!

Now for a crucified man to say anything would have been excruciatingly painful, but one of the words that Jesus managed to speak on the cross helps us to understand this whole ransom business a bit better. He cried out: *"It is finished!"* [52] The root word for that statement in Greek is 'Tetelestoi' which was a legal term, normally used when someone's debt had been paid off. It literally means 'paid in full.'

So what was Jesus "paying in full" on the cross?

Our ransom. And it cost Him everything – His very life.

But now His blood has paid it in full, the chains of slavery have been snapped to bits, and we can know the reality of true spiritual liberty and freedom from the soul-destroying, life-trashing effects of sin. We can know what it feels like to be set free, adopted and fully accepted into the awesome family of God.

Whoooppaah!!!

## ACCESS

ANYONE WHO COMES TO GOD THROUGH JESUS CAN HAVE FULL, DIRECT ACCESS INTO THE PRESENCE OF GOD.

So much cool stuff happened while Jesus was on the cross, but one of my favourites has got to be the ripping in half of the gigantic temple curtain clean. The curtain kept sinful people out of the 'Holy of Holies' where God's presence dwelt. In other words, it was a humungous signpost that said to "Access Denied", which was bad news for everyone! When Jesus' died, however, the torn-up curtain became a brand new signpost saying "Access All Areas." I love that. No one's excluded now – anyone who comes to God through Jesus can have full, direct access into the presence of God.

**OFFENSIVE**

That's immense!

**THERE'S NOTHING LEFT TO PAY!**

The blood of Jesus cleans all stains, breaks all chains, and makes us saints. The offer is open to absolutely anyone, it's completely free and there's nothing left to pay!

## HEALING

Back in the early 1990's American rock giants R.E.M released a single called 'Everybody Hurts.'

**THE CROSS WAS, IS, AND ALWAYS WILL BE GOOD NEWS FOR PEOPLE IN PAIN**

It struck a chord with millions of people because, like the lyric says: *"everybody hurts sometimes..."* [53]

Have you ever been hurt? You know – hurt deep down inside where words and even hugs don't reach? The answer is probably 'yes', because the truth is that most of us have (like the song says!) To be human is to hurt. That's what sin has done to us and to our world. Sadly, despite all the phenomenal wealth and technology that's around these days and is supposed to make our lives easier and happier, the reality is quite the opposite. There are currently record levels of people (especially youngsters) hating life, hating themselves and...hurting! Many are now so resigned to pain being 'the norm' that they've given-up on ever being free from it, and settled instead for just trying to numb it through drugs, therapy, self-harm, relationships, or whatever else offers a little bit or relief. That's why they call us 'the Prozac Generation', because oblivion doesn't hurt as much as reality. The trouble is, however, that the peace never lasts!

OK, now get this. No matter what pain you ever go through in this life – Christ crucified more than understands exactly where you're at and what you're going through! He really does. However, the miracle of the cross goes so much deeper than a God who simply understands...

It was around 750 BC(ish) when a Jewish prophet called Isaiah said some incredible stuff about Jesus and the sacrifice that He was going to make. One of the things he said was:

*"But He was pierced for our transgressions, He was crushed for our iniquities; the punishment that brought us peace was upon Him, and by His wounds we are healed."* [54]

At Calvary Jesus experienced the deepest levels of physical pain imaginable, but that was only a fraction of what He actually went through on the cross. In fact it was probably minimal compared to the emotional torment of betrayal, the humiliation of public disgrace, and the spiritual agony of His loving Father turning His face away from Him for the first time in eternity...

The cross was, is, and always will be good news for people in pain, because it tells us of the Saviour who suffered for all the stuff that damages us – guilt, regret, shame, anger, sickness, rejection, *everything!* Jesus took it all in our place so that we can be healed where it hurts!

That's the miracle message of the cross, and nothing and no one else in the universe can offer us that! It may sound too good to be true, but Christ crucified can do it – He's got the scars to prove it!

## LOVE

The gospel really is a message worth taking to the streets and shouting about. But there's still one vital part of our message that we haven't looked at yet. If we're not preaching it then we're not preaching the full Gospel. In fact without it there wouldn't be a Gospel at all!

The Gospel is all about God's love!

Whether by our families, our friends or our 'special' friends (who's the joker that just wolf-whistled?) we all want to know that we're loved! It's just in us! However, loads of people in the streets and cities around us right now feel anything but loved. Loneliness and self-hatred are rampant, especially among young people, many of whom have been badly hurt by people that claimed to love them. This is why the Gospel is seriously good news for those who are crying out for love:

*"But God demonstrates his own love for us in this: While we were still sinners, Christ died for us."* [55]

The cross says that there's a God who loves us!

WE'VE GOT A GOD WHO LITERALLY LOVES US TO DEATH!

For real!

Despite our sin problem.

Regardless of our failures.

He totally, utterly, passionately loves us!

More than we'll ever know and more than we even deserve.

We often think of love in terms of how much we deserve it (or not!) But God doesn't do love our way. The New Testament word for love is 'Agape' which is a rare Greek word describing a love that is rooted in the character of the one who loves, rather than in the worthiness of the person who is loved. In other words – God's love is all about Him wanting to love us, rather than whether or not we deserve it!

God doesn't just do love, God *is* love! [56]

Pure, perfect, selfless, never-failing, everlasting love!

It's in His DNA. It's what He's all about!

If you need proof – look no further than the cross. If actions really do speak louder than words, then *Christ crucified* screams *"I LOVE YOU!!!"* louder, more powerfully and more convincingly than anything else that's ever happened on this planet. The cross says that there's a God who loves us so much that He'd rather see His own Son Jesus go through the hell of crucifixion than spend eternity without us!

We've got a God who literally loves us to death!

# 3. Resurrection

JESUS' COMING BACK FROM THE DEAD IS ABSOLUTELY CENTRAL TO THE MESSAGE THAT WE PREACH.

*"Christ...was raised on the third day..."*

Have you ever heard someone preach a message like this:

*"God loves you so much that He sent Jesus to die for you on the cross. If you come to Jesus He'll forgive and get you into heaven!"*

I've heard and read that so many times that I've lost count, but it's not the full picture! If we're going to tell people to turn to Jesus, let's at least tell them that He's alive! Otherwise it's like telling them to trust a 2000 year-old corpse to save them – and that just sounds freakish!

While it's crucial to keep Christ crucified at the heart of our cross-driven message, for heaven's sake – let's not leave Him on the cross!!!

Here's the thing – If the cross was the end of the road for Jesus, and the end of the story for us, then we may as well forget about the cross-driven mission, and just spend the rest of our days eating, drinking and being merry before keeling over and pushing up a few daisies! Why? Because if Jesus only died, and then stayed dead – we should dismiss Him as a dangerous fake, a devious liar and someone to steer well clear of! Paul put it like this:

**"if Christ is not risen, then our preaching is empty and your faith is also empty."**[57]

Jesus' coming back from the dead is absolutely central to the message that we preach. Yes He had to die on the cross to sort out all that amazing stuff that we've just been looking at. But a dead Jesus can't save anyone! A dead Jesus = dead religion. And I for one am not going live, let alone die, for the dead religion of a dead god!

But Jesus isn't dead!

**OFFENSIVE**

HE'S ALIVE!!!

He rose again on the third day, just like He promised – and that's fantastic news for us and for our dying world.

It's a truth that's worth living for, a cause worth dying for, and a message worth shouting about!

## TRUTH-TELLER

Isaiah once cried out with a broken-heart *"truth is fallen in the street."* [58] If that was true 750 years ago, how true is it today? Truth hasn't so much fallen in the streets of the 21st century, as it's been viciously been gunned down.

It's hard to know who we can trust these days with countless reports of corruption amongst politicians and community leaders, sports stars breaking out of contracts if the money's right, marriages and families ripped apart by unfaithfulness, mistrust and broken promises, and even our own friends and loved ones stabbing us in the back. To be honest, I totally get what Pilate was on about when he asked Jesus that ancient post-modern question *"what is truth?"* [59] It's a question on many people's lips these days, as no one seems to know who or what to believe anymore, and that's an attitude that we'll encounter time after time on the cross-driven mission. We'll meet people who are sincerely asking questions like:

*"How do I know you're right?"*

*"All religions are the same – who says that Christianity is the only way?"*

*"Why should I believe Jesus rather than anyone else?"*

How do we answer questions like these? What's our gospel response?

See, they're perfectly reasonable questions to ask, because Jesus did make a lot of BIG promises and some MASSIVE claims about Himself. He made promises about God loving us and looking after us. About a day that's coming when justice and peace will be restored in the world and evil gets the kicking it's

long overdue. He promised us supernatural power to live for God in this world and He promised a place with Him in heaven when we die. He even said that He wasn't just the *only* way to God, but that He *is* God.

But how do we know that we can believe Him? How do we know that He's not just blagging? Basically, we need to look no further than His empty grave. Out of all the outrageous promises and bold claims that Jesus made, this one's got to be the daddy of them all:

*"The Son of Man…must be killed and after three days rise again."* [60]

Now anyone can make a statement like that, but to pull it off and actually rise from the dead – that's the sort of thing that only God can do. And that's what Jesus did! You can visit the grave of everyone who ever started a religion, because like every other sinful human – they either died, or will die. But Jesus isn't like everyone else. We need to be confident as we preach the good news to our confused world that all religion is dead, but Jesus is alive and He promises a life-changing, saving relationship with anyone who comes to Him.

There's an empty grave that says it's a promise He'll keep!

## DEATH-BEATER

It was about 11am when I got the worst phone call I've ever had to take:

*"Dai, it's your Mam. I've found a lump in my tummy and the doctor has admitted me to hospital for urgent surgery. It's too early to say yet, but there's a chance that it's cancer. We'll let you know as soon as we know anything."*

The next day our worst fears were confirmed – it was cancer. The doctors operated and removed a tumour the size of a football, but the cells had already spread to other organs inside her body. It was very serious. I went to visit her in hospital the next day and really didn't know what to expect. I guess I was expecting there to be a deathly atmosphere, a cold air of uncertainty and grief, coupled with the bitter tears of tragedy. But when I walked in, Mam was sat up in her bed with a massive smile spread right across her chops – and she was shining!

*"I've been reading Philippians."* was the only reason that she gave for the grace and peace that was just oozing out of her for all the world to see. I was completely blown away! I knew my Mam loved Jesus-she has

**JESUS HAS RIPPED THE TEETH OUT OF THE JAWS OF DEATH**

done since before I was born. But in that little room on that dark day, it all made sense in a completely new way! What is it that can give someone who was literally staring into the face of death such hope against all odds?

Jesus is alive!

Perhaps my sister's cat can help me explain...

My sister used to have a cat called Moggin, and you'll have to take my word for it – He was a gangster! He ruled our street with an iron claw, pulverising any cat that dared to tread on his turf, and assassinating mice, voles, shrews,(and various other assorted vermin) on a daily basis. He even dumped a severed bird-head on my sister's bedroom floor once (how mafia is that?!) He survived getting shot in the head by an air-gun, terrorised a boxer dog in our garden, and sliced my little finger open down to the bone (I've still got the scar!) Moggin was a killer (but I still kind of liked him!) Anyway, as Moggin got older, he started loosing teeth, and by the time he died, Moggin was no threat to anyone anymore, as his only chance of killing anything would have been by sucking it to death! Moggin had become a soft old pussy cat, which kind of reminds me of something that Paul wrote about the powerful significance of Jesus beating death and rising again:

*"**Death is swallowed up in victory.***
***O death where is your victory?***
***O death, where is your sting?***
*...**thanks be to God who gives us the victory through our LORD Jesus Christ.**"* [61]

Statistics are clear – 100% of people will eventually fall into the jaws of death, curl up their toes and die. But death likes to get a second bite – something the Bible calls the second death (which is basically hell forever). So many people around us these are scared to death of dying, and so they should be, because hell is a very real, intensely terrifying reality that awaits them. Tragically for them, this world is as close to heaven as they'll ever get – and that's a scary thought!

The good news of the gospel, however, is that by dying in our place, and then rising again, Jesus has ripped the teeth out of the jaws of death, so that we'll never have to worry about facing the horrors of hell. Just like Moggin the killer became Moggin the pussy cat, those who have turned to Jesus to save them can face the grave with no fear, knowing that this world is as close to hell as they'll ever get. That's why my mam could look the death square in eye and smile! It's almost like the closer she came to dying, the closer she came to Jesus and the more she shone.

## LIFE-GIVER

IF ANYONE EVER ASKS YOU "IF JESUS IS ALIVE, THEN WHERE'S HE AT RIGHT NOW?" TELL THEM STRAIGHT, "HE'S SORTING MY BEDROOM OUT!"

Living as I do in a small terraced house in the South Wales valleys, MTV Cribs always makes me laugh. Watching the rich and famous strutting around in their over-sized, over-priced gold-plated palaces, with more bedrooms than I've got pairs of pants and swimming pools bigger than the entire council estate I live on – it just tickles my chuckle muscle! Why? Because that's nothing compared to what we've got coming! Check out what Jesus is up to right now:

*"There are many rooms in my Father's home, and I am going to prepare a place for you...When everything is ready, I will come and get you, so that you will be with always be with me where I am."* [62]

If anyone ever asks you *"If Jesus is alive, then where's He at right now?"* Tell them straight, *"He's sorting my bedroom out!"* It might sound too good to be true but a day is coming when we get to leave the painful existence of living in this fractured world, and get the keys to a new, everlasting life in God's glorious paddock (heaven), and no crib on MTV even comes close. And check this out

– Jesus Himself is going to come and get us and give us a guided tour of the place! (Good job He's alive eh?!)

Check out what life's going to be like there:

*"I saw the holy city, new Jerusalem, coming down out of heaven from God, prepared as a bride adorned for her husband. And I heard a loud voice from the throne saying, 'Behold the dwelling place of God is with man. He will dwell with them, and they will be His people, and God Himself will be with them as their God. He will wipe every tear from their eyes, and death shall be no more, neither shall there be mourning nor crying nor pain anymore, for the former things have passed away."* [63]

This is the goal. The end of the cross-driven mission! I can't even begin to imagine how amazing everlasting life with Jesus is going to be. But I can't wait to find out either! What about you? Doesn't it sound like it's worth all the trouble? Worth all the pain? Worth hanging on for? Doesn't it sound like the sort of place you want others to get to experience? Me too – which is why we've got work to do!

Jesus alive.

He's still in the business of saving souls.

And we get to tell them about it.

# 4. Respond

As we saw right at the start of this chapter, at the heart of the cross-driven mission is the responsibility of sharing the gospel with others. I really hope that if nothing else, the stuff you've read here has filled you with a fresh wonder of the Gospel, and a brand-new passion for taking it to your world.

However, we need to be aware that preaching the gospel isn't merely a case of stating facts about what Jesus has done. Jesus-style preaching will always

> **THE GOAL OF THE CROSS-DRIVEN MISSION ISN'T TO GET PEOPLE TO STOP SINNING, IT'S TO SEE PEOPLE SAVED AND SET FREE FROM SIN.**

demand a response, as Jesus modelled perfectly for us in His first recorded sermon: *"repent and believe the Gospel."* [64]

We need to call people to repent! But don't worry, that's not as scary as it first sounds! The key to preaching repentance is simply *"speaking the truth in love."* [65]

'Repent' has got to be one of the most misunderstood Bible words ever! It's impossible to hear the word 'repent' without images coming to mind of some sweaty, Bible-thumping preacher screaming in people's faces that they're all going to hell and that if they don't want to go there, they need to fix themselves up, sort themselves out and stop doing all that bad stuff! We've all seen them, and most of us are at least a bit disturbed by them, if not completely terrified of them!

The good news for us, however, is that repentance is much more positive than that. In fact it's a uniquely revolutionary concept that speaks of grace, hope and heaven, not condemnation, judgement and hell. The Greek word for 'repent' is 'metanoeo' which means to 'turn' or to 'change one's mind'. The power of preaching repentance, however, depends entirely on where we place the emphasis.

If we are screaming at people telling them that they need to turn *from* their sinful lifestyle, what we are actually suggesting is that salvation is all about them, and that all they need to do is clean up their act a bit and God will like them! That's religious, death-inducing repentance (and is also an absolute load of pants!) We can't fix ourselves no matter how hard we try because our root problem's not what we do (sin) but who we are (sinners). The goal of the cross-driven mission isn't to get people to stop sinning, it's to see people saved and set free from sin. What's the point of trying to make ourselves look good on the outside, if we still stink on the inside? It's like Ali G once delicately said: *"I cannot polish a turd!"* [66] People can come off drugs, keep their pants on, stop cussing and even help old grannies across the road, but if their hearts remain unchanged they'll die in their sins and still end up in hell.

# OFFENSIVE ↻

True, life-giving repentance, on the other hand, involves urging people *to* turn to the God who permanently loves them despite how messed up they are. [67] To come as they are with no masks or pretences, bringing with them whatever doubts, fears and questions they may still have. To turn to the God who loved them enough to die for them, who rose again to give them real life, and who actually *wants* them to turn to Him.

To trust the God of grace to clean them up and radically change them from the inside out!

This is the kind of repentance that transforms lives and populates heaven.

## OFFENSIVE MORONIC DYNAMITE

As we step to where people are at and lovingly preach the cross-driven message to them, we have absolutely no control

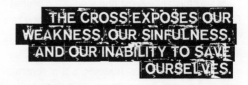

THE CROSS EXPOSES OUR WEAKNESS, OUR SINFULNESS, AND OUR INABILITY TO SAVE OURSELVES.

over how they will respond. However, we can be sure that they will respond in one of three ways:

 *"Jews demand miraculous signs and Greeks look for wisdom, but we preach Christ crucified: a stumbling block to Jews and foolishness to Gentiles, but to those whom God has called, both Jews and Greeks, Christ the power of God and the wisdom of God."* [68]

Religious people hate the message of Christ crucified. The Greek word for 'stumbling block' is 'skandalon' which is where we get the word 'scandalous' from (It can also be translated as 'offensive'). The message of the cross will always offend religious people because the root of religion is pride – *"I can save myself by my own efforts",* and the cross completely crushes pride, as it says *"When we were still powerless, Christ died for the ungodly."* [69]

The cross exposes our weakness, our sinfulness, and our inability to save ourselves. It's humbling and it's offensive, but it's the message that we've got to preach!

## THAT'S GOD'S DYNAMITE YOU'RE CARRYING!

Furthermore, Christ crucified is foolishness to brainiacs who are obsessed with their own wisdom and intelligence. The word 'foolishness' here comes from the Greek word 'moros', which is where we get the word 'moron' from. In other words, Christ crucified is a moronic message to those who are wise in their own eyes. To many the idea of God coming to earth only to die on a cross is totally stupid! That this gory death somehow represents God's greatest victory is completely absurd. That this blood-stained cross has opened up a way to heaven is nonsense. And that a crucified Christ is even worth a second thought is simply foolishness.

It's moronic!

But the cross of Jesus isn't moronic.

You're *not* a nutter!

You need to believe that with all your heart, as people laugh, mock and patronise you for passionately proclaiming a message that, as far as they're concerned, makes you a brain-dead idiot for believing it!

Now If Christ crucified is so scandalous and so foolish to so many, you've got to wonder why it's the message that God's given us to preach! Surely He could have come up with something a bit more politically correct than this! It offends religious pride and insults human intelligence. But here's the thing – it's also seriously powerful. The Greek word for power is 'dunamis' and it's the word we get 'dynamite' from! I love that. God hasn't just given us some weak, foolish message that doesn't work.

That's God's dynamite you're carrying!

# OFFENSIVE ⚡

## THE AFTERMATH

# GARETH'S STORY

" I'd always believed that the Gospel is the most powerful message there is. I also always believed it's what everyone needed to hear and that I had a responsibility to tell them. Unfortunately though, after one or two failed attempts at sharing the Gospel in school I just got discouraged and got into a mindset that there was no point trying anymore. Praise God that when I started thinking like that I did the Offensive course.

Offensive was the wake-up call I needed. I was reminded again of the power of the gospel and I was challenged to take it out to the people of this world who need it so badly! (Just like I did before I heard it!) I was inspired to be a revolutionary for Christ and encouraged that God was still willing and able to use me on his mission!

Since Offensive I've had so many fresh opportunities to proclaim the love of Jesus, whether in the simple form of conversations with friends in college, or speaking to a room full of young people at New Wine Cymru. I've been insanely blessed by how God has used me and I believe that he will continue to use me (and trust me if he can use me he can use you!). God really used the offensive course to get me out of the rut I was in.

I just thank Him that he's now using me to spread his awesome message!

# CHAPTER THREE

## FIGHTING ON OUR FACES

"ALL OUR STRENGTH LIES IN PRAYER." [70]

- C.H SPURGEON

## SECRET WEAPON

In 1969, Walt Disney released a fun little film called 'Herbie – The Love Bug.' It was the first of several motion pictures that tell the story of Herbie – a plucky VW Beetle, who was unstoppable both on and off the racetrack. In fact, despite his apparently lowly status, Herbie was able to run rings around everyone and everything that he came up against, busting crazy stunts, saving the day and generally having a lot more fun than your average car!

However, it may come as a shock for you to learn that the adventures of Herbie are not rooted in reality. (Cars aren't alive and they don't actually have personalities!) Nevertheless there was still a lot more to Herbie's incredible speed and stunt antics than first met the eye. He might have looked ordinary to everyone else, but Herbie possessed a potent secret weapon – a powerful Porsche 356 Turbo engine that had been neatly fitted into the engine space at the rear of the car, allowing him to pull wheelies and propelling him to reach speeds of up to 132mph! There was a serious amount of power in there, but it was well hidden underneath his bog-standard bonnet!

When Jesus first showed up on the scene, on the surface He would have looked like any other random Rabbi walking around the

**PRAYERLESS PREACHING IS POWERLESS AND INEFFECTIVE.**

dusty streets of Galilee. However, as He started to preach the good news and stretch out His hand of mercy it soon became clear that there was a lot more to Him than His humble appearance suggested.

Jesus had a secret weapon:

*"While it was still night, way before dawn, he got up and went out to a secluded spot and prayed."*[71]

Jesus prayed.

That was His secret weapon! As the Son of God He had all the resources of heaven at His disposal, yet He still saw the need to get up, get out and make time and space for private prayer. Now if Jesus saw the value of spending quality time with His Father in prayer, we would do well to learn from the master missionary Himself and follow His example! Of course we need to be out there preaching the gospel, but prayer is where the power's at!

Prayerless preaching is powerless and ineffective. We need to make sure that the words we speak are completely saturated in prayer – otherwise we'll just be firing blanks!

## ON YOUR KNEES

Back in 1888, a Canadian missionary couple called Jonathan and Rosalind Goforth set out on a pioneering adventure to take the Gospel to the unreached millions of China's Henan province. Already on the mission-field in China was the inspirational James Hudson Taylor, who wrote them a letter with this advice:

*"Brother, if you would enter that province, you must go forward on your knees."*

Obviously he wasn't encouraging the Goforths to shuffle their way across the border like a pair of missionary midgets, burning holes in their knee-caps in the name of the LORD! What he was actually doing was encouraging them to recognise that if they were going to successfully reach and rescue the lost people of Henan, they needed to grab hold of God's secret weapon and pray!

Now in an age when evangelistic trends and techniques are changing more quickly than David Beckham's hair-cut, prayer might not be the most exciting or attractive mission method out there, but Taylor had been around long enough to know just how crucial prayer is in the cross-driven mission. The truth is that we can get so caught up in trying to stay up to speed with all the latest ways of 'doing mission', that we end up distracted, dazed, and disconnected from the One who it's all about in the first place. Taylor put it like this:

*"We have given too much attention to methods and to machinery and to resources, and too little to the Source of Power, the filling of the Holy Ghost."*

This chapter is all about rediscovering the ultimate method for mission! I could try to write yet another trendy master-piece on the latest way to win the world for Jesus, but I'd rather just inspire you to get on your knees with a heart full of faith, and discover for yourself that tapping in to the super-power-source of the Holy Spirit, through prayer, is the ultimate key to the cross-driven mission.

## WALKIE-TALKIE

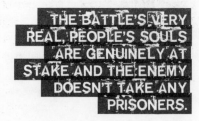

THE BATTLE'S VERY REAL, PEOPLE'S SOULS ARE GENUINELY AT STAKE AND THE ENEMY DOESN'T TAKE ANY PRISONERS.

We don't know exactly what Jesus prayed about on this particular occasion, but Jesus was a prayer warrior and the Gospels are absolutely packed with lessons and examples that He's given us in the art of prayer warfare! This chapter is going to explore what it means to pray 'the Jesus way', but firstly, if all this talk of secret weapons, prayer warriors and warfare all sounds a bit too militant for you, can I remind you that we're in a war-zone. We weren't saved to enjoy a holy holiday as we wait for the bus to heaven, we were recruited as members of God's global gospel rescue team. The battle's very real, people's souls are genuinely at stake and the enemy doesn't take any prisoners. Which is why I love John Piper's definition of prayer:

*"Prayer is primarily a wartime walkie-talkie for the mission of the church as it advances against the powers of darkness and unbelief....Until you know that life is war, you cannot know what prayer is for: Prayer is for the accomplishment of a wartime mission."* [72]

Prayer connects us to God! It's how we communicate with Him as we jump out of the trenches to pull casualties to eternal

**PRAYER CONNECTS US TO GOD!**

safety. No soldier would dare step out of the trenches without a strategy from HQ, and in the same way, prayer is how we tune in to God to receive His orders, and how we keep in touch with Him in the heat of battle. Staying connected to God is so crucial to the rescue mission that Oswald Chambers went so far as to say that *"Prayer is not a preparation for the battle, it is the battle."* [73] If that's true, and we want to successfully complete our part of the mission – we need to stay connected.

# TIME, SPACE & SACRIFICE

**REGULAR TIME WITH GOD IN THE SECRET PLACE IS COSTLY**

As part of His 'Sermon On The Mount' series, Jesus taught us how to pray. However, just before teaching what is probably the most famous prayer ever, Jesus also dished out this advice:

*"when you pray, go into your room, and when you have shut your door, pray to your Father who is in the secret place;"* [74]

This is why Jesus had got up early and gone somewhere quiet – He didn't want anything to distract Him from prayer. Back in those days the religious leaders would regularly stand on busy street corners and try to impress everyone with their big, fancy prayers. Jesus was totally against the idea of praying to impress others (religion). He was much more about simply spending quality time with His loving Father (relationship).

If we're going to learn how to pray the Jesus way, it's going to take discipline. We live in a hectic world where we are surrounded by people and things that are constantly vying for our attention. In the middle of it all, we need to find a way of creating space every day to take time out and meet our God in the secret place. That may be in your bedroom, in your car, in a local park, or in some other quiet place. It may be first thing in the morning, during your dinner break or last thing at night. The time and place is not really what matters here. What's important is a deep-down desire to spend time with your Father.

However, regular time with God in the secret place is costly. It may not cost you financially, but you may need to roll back the duvet and crawl out of bed an hour earlier than you'd like. Or you may need to miss a meal, give up a hobby or reassess your social life. Could you do that? Are you willing to make such personal sacrifices in order to spend some precious time in intimate relationship with your Father?

If so, then you're in the right place to pray like you've never prayed before. Here's how Jesus suggests we start:

*"Our Father in heaven,*
*Hallowed be Your name.*
*Your kingdom come.*
*Your will be done*
*On earth as it is in heaven.*
*Give us this day our daily bread.*
*And forgive us our debts,*
*As we forgive our debtors.*
*And do not lead us into temptation,*
*But deliver us from the evil one.*
*For Yours is the kingdom and the power and the glory forever.*
*Amen."* [75]

# 1. Relationship

*"Our Father in heaven.."*

OK, let's be clear here – prayer is not a magic formula, or some kind of cold-blooded ritual that we have to go to

**PRAYER IS ROOTED IN RELATIONSHIP**

through in order to prove to God that we mean business. Prayer is rooted in relationship. Jesus prayed to His Father and encourages us to do the same. The only way that we can do that is by coming through Jesus, because as He said *"No one can come to the Father except through me."* [76] Jesus' rescue mission ultimately led Him to the cross, where something sensational happened – we got adopted!

*"God sent [Jesus] to buy freedom for us who were slaves to the law, so that He could adopt us as his very own children. And because we are His children, God has sent the Spirit of His Son into our hearts, prompting us to call out, "Abba, Father." Now you are no longer a slave but God's own child. And since you are His child, God has made you His heir."* [77]

Wow!!! Stop and think about that for a minute because that's just immense!

There's so much more to the word 'Abba' than just a cheesy Swedish pop group from the 70's! Abba is the Aramaic word for 'Father', or to be more precise 'Daddy!' It's a word that speaks of love, intimacy and security.

If you're a Christian – God in heaven is now your Dad.

Now I'm more than aware that for some, the concept of knowing and enjoying God as Father is far from easy, as many have had to grow up without a father-figure in their life at all, or have suffered greatly at the hands of cruel and abusive men. If that's you, I am truly sorry! However, it's crucial that you understand and believe that Father God's not like that! He's perfect, pure, patient and compassionate. He's *"slow to anger and abounding in steadfast love"* [78] He promises to be *"A father to the fatherless"* [79] and He keeps His promises. God doesn't want you to live in fear, but to learn to trust and lean on Him for everything. God is a Father who craves spending time with His kids. He's never too busy to listen and never too cold to care.

Getting a right understanding of our relationship with God as Father is essential if we're going to fully get to grips with the secret weapon of prayer. See, to God we're not just pawns in a game, or insignificant statistics. We mean everything to Him! Our Father is passionate about us, and as we press on with the cross-driven mission, we go as His precious children, with instant, access to Him always available.

# 2. Glory

*"Hallowed be Your name..."*

THERE'S ONLY ONE SUPERSTAR ON THIS MISSION – AND THAT'S JESUS CHRIST HIMSELF!

We live in days when fame is everything. Currently, the top response among young people to the question *"What do you want to be when you grow up?"* is *"I want to be famous!"* From X-Factor hopefuls to the freaks on Big Brother, and streakers on cup-final day – it seems like people will go anywhere and do anything for their 5 minutes in the spotlight! The pursuit of *"check-me-out"* fame at all costs is now a social epidemic!

The cross-driven mission, however, represents a lifestyle that is the complete opposite of that. We live, breathe, preach and pray in order to make God famous! To

**THE PASSIONATE PURSUIT OF GOD'S GLORY MUST BE OUR PRIMARY FOCUS AS WE PRAY!**

make Him look good and make others say *"Woah! Check Him out!"* We exist to spread the glory of God right across the world. Jesus told us to pray that God's name would be *"hallowed"* (set apart as holy and awesome!). If that's what Jesus was all about, it's surely what we should be all about too!

We need to wake up and smell the coffee – God doesn't need us, He doesn't depend on us, and He isn't obsessed about making us famous, regardless of who we are or what we've got to offer. There's only one superstar on this mission – and that's Jesus Christ Himself! Perhaps we need to learn a quick lesson from OT bad-boy Jonah who, while sloshing around in puke and juice in the belly of a giant fish, came out with this little nugget:

**"Salvation belongs to the LORD."** [80]

This is without doubt one of the most liberating truths that I've ever learned: That I am not God's gift to this world – Jesus is! That I am weak, puny, pathetic and couldn't even save myself, let alone anyone else – but God is **"mighty to save."** [81] We need to humble ourselves, because the minute we think that we have anything to offer this world other than Jesus – we get proud, we get weak, and our mission's in danger of failing!

That's why as God's commandos we fight facedown in prayer. Prayer is recognition of our absolute dependence on Him in everything! Facedown soldiers embrace their own weakness and take Jesus at His word when He said: **"My grace is all you need. My power works best in weakness."** [82] Facedown soldiers are unstoppable, as Jim Elliot once said: *"That saint who advances on his knees never retreats."* Facedown soldiers don't get side-tracked by chasing glory for themselves, they just humbly pray that God would work through them to save others, and then make sure that He gets all the credit for it too.

The passionate pursuit of God's glory must be our primary focus as we pray! Spurgeon put it like this: *"This is the way to pray; when thy prayers seek God's glory, it is God's glory to answer thy prayers."* [83]

# 3. Kingdom

*"Your kingdom come."*

**OUR PRIMARY RESPONSE TO ALL THE TRAGEDY AND PAIN THAT SURROUNDS US TODAY SHOULD BE PASSIONATE PRAYER FOR GOD'S KINGDOM TO COME IN FORCE.**

It was around 1000BC when the Book of Judges was written. It's a hard-hitting, gritty account of how messed-up things get when God's people turn their back on Him and decide to do life their own way. The book closes with the chilling words:

*"In those days Israel had no king; all the people did whatever seemed right in their own eyes."* [84] Watch the news, read the paper, or open your front door today, and see what happens when people do 'whatever seems right in their own eyes.' It's carnage out there! As we look around at a world that's being ripped apart by poverty, injustice and the vicious consequences of sin, we need to understand that the root cause of it all is a universal rejection of God as King (Genesis 3). The tragedy is that God's not a cruel or oppressive King, but an unstoppably good One. Check it out:

*"Your throne, O God, will last for ever and ever; a scepter of justice will be the scepter of your kingdom."* [85]

Where God's on the throne, justice prevails! Where people reject His rule – injustice, sin and death prevail. It's that simple. However, unwilling to leave us to self-destruct, God in His mercy promised that He would send the King of kings into the world (Jesus) who would step up and put things right once and for all. So when Jesus popped up on the radar centuries later, it's really not surprising that He talked a lot about the kingdom of God.

Amongst other things, Jesus urged us to pray "Your kingdom come." The word for 'come' is the Greek word 'Erchomai' which can mean to arise, emerge, or to be established. Put simply, Jesus was encouraging us to pray that

**WE NEED TO GET URGENT AND PLEAD WITH GOD TO HAVE MERCY ON THE PEOPLE AROUND US, WHOEVER THEY ARE AND WHATEVER STATE THEY'RE IN.**

the justice, righteousness, peace and grace that characterise God and His kingdom, would advance and take root right across our world. Therefore, our primary response to all the tragedy and pain that surrounds us today should be passionate prayer for God's kingdom to come in force. For a flood of justice and mercy to sweep away all that's gone before, and for Jesus alone to be worshipped as King!

However, while Jesus would encourage us all to get on our knees and pray with a wide-angle lens for God's kingdom to come globally, He'd also suggest that we need to narrow our focus too:

*"I tell you the truth, no one can see the kingdom of God unless he is born again"*[86]

A kingdom is made up of individuals, and Jesus clearly stated that the only way that our friends, family and workmates are ever going to see, and ultimately belong to God's kingdom, is if they're born-again. They need to be saved! That means that we need to get urgent and plead with God to have mercy on the people around us, whoever they are and whatever state they're in.

One of the most helpful tools that I've ever come across for praying for people is the Ignition card. [87] It's basically a small card that has space for you to write the names of 3 people that you're crying out to God for, with the challenge to *"Keep on praying"* [88] at the bottom. Whether you use it as a bookmark, stick it in your wallet or on the back of your toilet door, it's a simple, practical way to help you pray for others!

## WHEN WE PRAY, PEOPLE GET SAVED, AND GOD'S KINGDOM DRAWS THAT LITTLE BIT CLOSER!

## TEARS

Crying out for God's kingdom to come can be painful, emotional and draining:

*"If we are engaged with the world around us, then we will care about that world. We will be passionate about people's needs, our holiness and God's glory. We will not be still in prayer. We will cry out for mercy with a holy violence. If we are silent it will be because in our distress, words have failed us."* [89]

A couple of years ago, my wife and I took our gorgeous baby girl out on her first ever dog walk around the streets of the council estate where we were living. As we rounded a corner, we were horrified to see two boys (12 and 14) who we knew well and loved deeply, dancing around the garden with glasses of vodka, totally off their faces. What was so heart-breaking was seeing the 'adult' of the house leaning out of the window with a bottle to top them up! It was just messed-up! My initial instinct was *"I need to get my baby home – I don't want her to see this."* My wife's reaction was much more profound – she stopped where she was and burst into tears. *"This is wrong. This is wrong. This can't happen!!!"* was about all she could say! I eventually persuaded her to go home with the baby and the dog, and I sat down on the pavement literally trembling in prayer.

The next hour is still a blur, but to summarise – it involved a family argument, a rottweiler attacking a small child, a kitchen knife, a teenager collapsing in panic, a girl swinging a golf-club at her step-dad, a 5 year old sobbing his heart out, and me sat on a kerb, comforting him and praying for the 14 year old. When I eventually got home I literally collapsed in a flood of tears! When you're hungry for God's kingdom to come, stuff like that just breaks your heart! And if it breaks your heart, you can be sure it breaks God's!!! Jesus Himself was no stranger to tears! [90]

Praise God that this story's got a happy ending. That 14 year old boy came to see us the next day with a whole load of God-questions that had been triggered off by the events of the day before. We spent several hours with him, gave him a Bible and prayed for him. 2 weeks later, he sat on our sofa and prayed that Jesus would come into his life and save him! Come on!!!

*"Those who sow in tears, will reap with songs of joy!"* [91]

When we pray, people get saved, and God's Kingdom draws that little bit closer!

# 4. Will.

*"Your will be done on earth as it is in heaven..."*

BEFORE DOING OR SAYING ANYTHING, JESUS TOOK TIME TO PRAY

I got in a taxi recently, and was completely unprepared for what happened next...

I told the driver where to go (not in a rude way!), sat back in my seat and relaxed, until all of a sudden, out of nowhere I heard someone scream out *"take the next \*<%!~^# turning left!"* I freaked out!!! After a couple of deep breaths (and a rapid change of underwear) the taxi driver explained to me that he had just installed an Ozzy Osborne satellite navigation system in his cab, which basically meant that by combining a high-tech satellite system (that I don't even pretend to understand!) with the vulgar rantings of Mr.Osborne (that I don't even want to understand!) he could drive his taxi pretty much anywhere in the world, without ever opening a map! All he had to do was type in the desired destination and follow the directions! Nuts!!!

When Jesus stepped down to earth, He had absolutely no doubt about where He was heading. Time after time He explained that: *"The Son of Man is going to be betrayed into the hands of men. They will kill him, and on the third day he will be raised to life."* [92] He knew that His entire life pointed to the cross, and nothing was going to knock Him off course! However, His journey to the cross was far from straight forward, with all sorts of crazy twists, turns and stop-offs along the way. How did Jesus know where to go and what to do? Was He just on cruise control or was there more to it than that? These are important questions, because as we crack on with the cross-driven mission, the temptation can be to just go wherever, and do whatever feels right. How do we find out what we *should* be doing?

**IF WE'RE GOING TO PRAY LIKE THIS, IT'S ESSENTIAL THAT WE'RE TOTALLY WILLING TO SUBMIT TO GOD'S PLAN FOR US**

We need to pray the Jesus way.

Jesus once said: *"I have come down from heaven, not to do my own will, but the will of Him who sent me."* [93] He went on to say: *"the Son...only what he sees the Father doing."* [94] and *"The Father who sent me has commanded me what to say and how to say it."* [95]

That's staggering! Before doing or saying anything, Jesus took time to pray: *"Father, what are you up to here? Where do I fit in? What do you want me to do? What should I say?"* Or in simpler terms: *"Your will be done."*

In heaven, God's will reigns supreme. By praying that God's perfect will be done down here as it is in heaven, we're asking God to get us involved with all the amazing stuff that He's up to. It might be that God tells you to do something relatively small, like go and talk to someone on the bus, because that person's really on His heart. Or it could be something massive like sell your house and go live in another country that's crying out for the gospel! The truth is you'll never know if you're not listening!

Seeking out God's perfect plan in prayer, and letting Him type His desired destination into our sat nav each day, will always lead us to the right place, with the right words for the right people at the right time! And that's a seriously exciting place to be!

However, if we're going to pray like this, it's essential that we're totally willing to submit to God's plan for us. We need to hold our own visions, dreams, desires and 'rights' in an open hand, in order to make His purposes our priority. And that can hurt, as Jesus' journey to the cross reminds us! When Jesus taught people how to pray like this, He was still the local superstar. However, the next time He prayed *"your will be done"* it was in Gethsemane Garden as He sweat blood shortly before His betrayal and arrest. The cross was without doubt God's master-plan for saving the world, but Jesus still had to walk it through.

Wherever it takes you and whatever it costs you, if you're willing to pray *"your will be done on earth as it is in heaven"*, then strap yourself in and get ready for the ride of your life!

# 5. Help

*"Give us this day our daily bread."*

Something that I really used to struggle with was the idea that if life's all about God and His glory, then I should only be praying about that, so coming to Him with a shopping list of stuff that I needed was selfish and sinful!

> **BEING HUMBLE ENOUGH TO ACCEPT THAT WE NEED ANYTHING, AND TRUSTING GOD TO SORT US OUT, ACTUALLY GIVES HIM GREAT GLORY**

I've since come to learn that that's a completely wrong understanding of what God's like and how prayer works! Being humble enough to accept that we need *anything*, and trusting God to sort us out, actually gives Him great glory, as John Piper testifies:

*"Prayer is the open admission that without Christ we can do nothing...Prayer humbles us as needy, and exalts God as wealthy."* [96]

Jesus encourages us to shamelessly pray for help: *"give us this day our daily bread."* Remember that prayer is rooted in relationship with a loving Father, a truth that prompted Jesus to later say: *"Which of you, if his son asks for bread, will give him a stone? Or if he asks for a fish, will give him a snake? If you, then, though you are evil, know how to give good gifts to your children, how much more will your Father in heaven give good gifts to those who ask him!"* [97]

Now I'm a dad who's absolutely besotted with his kids, and I'd sooner chew my own leg off than ever see them go without!!! If that's the level of an imperfect dad's love for his kids, how much stronger is God's love going to be?! However, note that we're not advised to pray *"give us this day our daily lollipop."* Bread is something that we all need. Lollipops aren't! In other words, we shouldn't treat God like a glorified vending machine, sticking in a few prayers and expecting Him to sort us out with whatever treats we fancy. Rather, Jesus wants to just reassure us that God's got our backs, that He knows what's best, and that if we need stuff – we shouldn't be shy in asking for it.

**NO MATTER HOW GREAT OUR NEED, OR HOW BLEAK OUR SITUATION MAY SEEM, WE CAN ALWAYS PRAY FOR HELP WITH CONFIDENCE**

The cross-driven mission is the perfect setting to learn how to pray for help. Whether it's seeking wisdom for the next step (James 1v5), or comfort in the heat of battle (James 5v13). If it's praying for God to open doors (Colossians 4v3), for the courage to speak up (Acts 4v23-31), or for back-up in the trenches (Matthew 9v38), God's always the best person to turn to. Therefore, no matter how great our need, or how bleak our situation may seem, we can always pray for help with confidence because:

*"You can be sure that God will take care of everything you need, His generosity exceeding even yours in the glory that pours from Jesus."* [98]

Whatever else we need, we need to be on our knees!

# 6. Connection

*"And forgive us our debts, as we forgive our debtors."*

Mobile phones are great – but only when they work! Not many things are as annoying as screaming down the phone at someone who can't hear a word that you're saying because there's no signal! In the same way, if prayer really is the secret weapon of mission then it's crucial that we don't lose our signal to heaven. The thing is, it can sometimes feel like God's just not there, or He's not listening. Like your prayers are just bouncing straight back at you and that God's either unwilling or unable to respond. Can you relate to that? If so, then check out what God's got to say about it:

*"Surely the arm of the LORD is not too short to save, or his ear too dull to hear. But your iniquities have separated you from your God; your sins have hidden his face from you, so that he will not hear."* [99]

# OFFENSIVE ⟳

The problem's not on God's end of the line – the problem's with us! Our sin disconnects us from God!

**OUR SIN DISCONNECTS US FROM GOD!**

Martin Smith once penned the powerful lyrics *"Forgive us all, forgive us please, as we fight for this broken world on our knees!"* [100] That cry perfectly captures the heart of Jesus as He urges us to pray *"forgive us our debts."* Forgiveness isn't just something that those lot out there need – we still need it too! And as God told King Solomon, it's when His people turn to Him for forgiveness that true revival's just round the corner:

*"if My people who are called by My name humble themselves, and pray and seek my face and turn from their wicked ways, then I will hear from heaven and will forgive their sin and heal their land."* [101]

The good news is that we've got a God who loves to forgive and who wants to stay connected to us at all costs. Therefore, whatever sins have cut us off from Him, we can take them to the cross, fully confident that: *"If we confess our sins, he is faithful and just to forgive us our sins and to cleanse us from all unrighteousness."* [102]

One of the worst things that can happen to us on the cross-driven mission is to lose sight of our own need of a Saviour! If we're going to effectively fight for this broken world on our knees, we need to stay connected, which is why keeping the cross at the centre of all we do is so crucial.

## PAY IT FORWARD

Jesus also wants us to understand that we've been forgiven so that we too can then pass on the blessing of forgiveness to others. It's a bit like what little Trevor McKinney came up with in the film Pay It Forward, when he decided that the best way to respond to someone's kindness is not to pay them back, but to pay it forward to someone else! Jesus taught us to pray: *"forgive us our debts, as we forgive our debtors"* because the two go hand-in-hand! If He was willing to forgive us, we should be looking for opportunities to share that forgiveness with others?

IF HE WAS WILLING TO FORGIVE US, WE SHOULD BE LOOKING FOR OPPORTUNITIES TO SHARE THAT FORGIVENESS WITH OTHERS?

Jesus even taught us to *"love your enemies and pray for those who persecute you,"* [103] something He modelled perfectly at the cross as He prayed forgiveness for the men who brutally killed Him.

Forgiving our enemies is one of the toughest things to do, but it's as people are hating us, slagging us off and beating us up, that our true understanding of the cross will really shine through. We'll either retaliate sinfully and fight fire with fire, or we'll recognise that because of His amazing grace to us, we're in the perfect position to pay it forward! There's no answer to that kind of prayer-power, and if you can pray like that for your enemies – you can pray for anyone!

Forgiven saints should be forgiving saints. And forgiving saints are unstoppable on their knees!

# 7. Protection

*"And do not lead us into temptation, but deliver us from the evil one."*

How's this for a cheery thought – we've got a savage enemy who hates our God, hates our mission, and hates our guts:

*"Stay alert! Watch out for your great enemy, the devil. He prowls around like a roaring lion, looking for someone to devour."* [104]

One of the ways that the devil wants to take us out of the cross-driven mission is by tempting us to sin – destroying our communication with God, cutting off our supplies and leaving us stranded like sitting ducks! If prayer is how we wage war, temptation is without doubt the enemy's weapon of choice. We all face temptation in all sorts of ways on a regular basis, and it sucks! However, while we should expect it, we certainly shouldn't desire it, and the good news is that Jesus has taught us how to be bullet-proof in prayer:

*"do not lead us into temptation, but deliver us from the evil one."*

# OFFENSIVE

Here's some of the artillery that the evil one will inevitably use to try to gun us down:

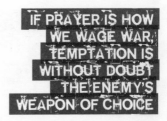
IF PRAYER IS HOW WE WAGE WAR, TEMPTATION IS WITHOUT DOUBT THE ENEMY'S WEAPON OF CHOICE

When the mission's going smoothly – we get tempted to relax. When things are tough – we get tempted to quit. When we're burnt-out – we get tempted to slack-off. When things seem slack – we get tempted to make ourselves busy. When people praise us – we get tempted to be proud. When people hate us – we get tempted to value their opinion more than God's. When we feel weak – we get tempted to compromise. And when we've blown it again – we get tempted to believe the lie that God won't forgive us.

We don't have to take any of those bullets! Jesus Himself was tempted by the devil, but He stood strong. Therefore, when we pray, we're coming to the One who's got what it takes to get us through:

*"For we do not have a high priest who is unable to sympathize with our weaknesses, but we have one who has been tempted in every way, just as we are – yet was without sin. Let us then approach the throne of grace with confidence, so that we may receive mercy and find grace to help us in our time of need."* [105]

**WHEN WE PRAY, WE'RE COMING TO THE ONE WHO'S GOT WHAT IT TAKES TO GET US THROUGH**

Whatever Satan fires at us, let's just use it as an excuse to turn to God for help! Let's point the devil to the cross where His death warrant was signed, then point him to the lake of fire where His death sentence will be served! He might strut round like a lion, but if we resist him in Christ, he'll scarper like a little pussycat with his tail between his legs!

See, the devil's not scared of us one little bit. But he's scared to death of Jesus Christ, and when we get serious in prayer, we're bringing Him into the fight – and there's only One winner there! Prayer literally is an offensive weapon, which is probably why someone once said: *"Satan laughs at our toiling, mocks at our wisdom, but trembles when we pray!"* [106]

Prayer really does make us bullet-proof!

# 8. Break-Through

*"For Yours is the kingdom and the power and the glory forever. Amen."*

Fighting on our faces isn't easy. There's much more comfortable places to be than on our knees, admitting our limitations, confronting our weaknesses, confessing our sins, breaking our pride and seeking God's will no matter what the cost. But it's completely worth it! Why? Jesus would put it like this:

**"For Yours is the kingdom and the power and the glory forever."**

That's what it's all about, or should I say that's who it's all about! This whole cross-driven mission is about God's magnificent kingdom rolling on. It's about His power being displayed in spectacular ways in unlikely places. It's about His glory being seen by everyone, and His Name being honoured forever!

**GET DESPERATE, GET PASSIONATE AND GET ON YOUR KNEES.**

And He's called us to be part of it! That just blows me away! However, if we're going to succeed on this mission, we need to follow Christ's example. He got on His knees – we need to do the same!

See I don't know about you, but I'm more desperate than ever to see God flex His mercy-muscles and break through into the broken lives of people all around me in this increasingly savage and tragic world. To see them radically saved and set free, to witness homes, streets, cities and nations rebuilt in the name of Jesus is something that I just dream about! If you're with me on that, then take this chapter seriously. Don't just read it, nod in agreement and then carry on as normal.

Get desperate, get passionate and get on your knees.

" As a young Christian, I was always being told about how essential prayer was. I found that this was very true during the Offensive course, as I came to know that the work of God could not be done without first consulting the one in charge; God himself.

On the Summer Offensive mission in Cardiff, prayer helped me to prepare my heart, mind, soul and body each day before going out to do outreach and prayer kept me going throughout the day. It was amazing to talk to God in such a constant and real way. It was also amazing to hear him speaking to me, prompting my heart and giving me spiritual eyes to see where I was needed.

Prayer is a powerful tool and so it's no surprise that we are told to do it countless times in the bible. Being active in my prayer life during Offensive drove the way to an active prayer life when I later went on a mission-trip to Argentina. I was able to commit the work and myself fully to God and I learned to trust him, knowing that he knew the circumstances and that he had the solution. Through prayer, I was able to grow closer to God.

He drew near to me as I drew near to him. It was awesome! "

# CHAPTER FOUR

## FUEL FOR THE FLAMES

"THE LOVE OF CHRIST COMPELS US." [107]

- APOSTLE PAUL

I learned some pretty cool stuff from my dad as I was growing up:

How to jump off cliffs.

How to climb back up them again.

How (and why) to throw slippers at the TV whenever Margaret Thatcher was on.

How to decapitate chickens.

Where the phrase *"running around like a headless chicken"* came from.

And how to chop wood.

Fair play to my old man, he knows more about hacking trees apart than any beaver (you should see his collection of axes, chainsaws and other gruesome tools), which is just as well because we had an open wood fire in the house, which was both a curse and a blessing. It was a curse because wood fires need wood to work (sounds basic I know), so dad used to drag me up mountains, down rivers and through forests to chop up trees and chuck them in the trailer. Then I'd have to carry them all around the back of the house to store them while he put his feet up and had a cuppa (at least that's how I remember it!) However, the curse was soon forgotten when the winter set in and we lit the fire in the house. I soon learned to appreciate fire.

But it also fascinated me because it's such a crazy thing!

Like...what is it?!

It burns things down, lights stuff up, melts iron and purifies gold. It fascinates naughty kids, destroys entire forests and yet warms our homes and drives the engines of all sorts of vehicles from petrol scooters to jumbo jets!

Fire rocks!

But what the Dickens is it?!

Wikipedia (the online source of all knowledge) defines it like this:

*"Fire is a form of combustion. Most typically, the word fire refers to the combination of the brilliant glow and large amount of heat released during a rapid, self-sustaining exothermic oxidation process of combustible gases ejected from a fuel."* [108]

Which all sounds a bit scientific and technical to me. Perhaps a more simple way of putting it would be something like this:

*"Fire is what happens when heat or some other type of energy is mixed with something that burns (fuel). It creates a gas that lights and heats stuff up (flames)."* [109]

Question: What all that's that go to do with the Gospel?

Answer: Loads!

## BURNING BONES

Why is it that whenever good stuff happens to us we just have to tell someone else about it? Exam results, success in sports, getting engaged, baby's first burp, whatever: *"Listen up – I've just got to tell you this…"*

Why? Because good news is worth spreading!

In the Old Testament there was a prophet called Jeremiah who lived in some pretty dark days, when everyone seemed to hate God and anything to do with Him. (Sound familiar?) Jeremiah was literally one of the only people on the planet at that time who cared about living and standing for God, and he was convinced that God's news is good news. Now back then God's message wasn't a podcast that most people were subscribing to, but nothing was going to shut Jeremiah up. Something was burning hot inside him and it wasn't vindaloo:

**OFFENSIVE**

*"His word burns in my heart like a fire. It's like a fire in my bones! I am worn out trying to hold it in! I can't do it!"* [110]

When you first experienced God's outrageous grace, forgiveness, healing and all that other amazing stuff in your own life – come on, you must have wanted to scream your head off about it, because good news spreads – like wildfire!

*"LISTEN UP – I'VE JUST GOT TO TELL YOU THIS..."*

Jeremiah couldn't get away from God's word. It had literally burned itself into his very core and there was no way he could keep it to himself! If he tried zipping his lips it just wore him out – the fire was burning out of control (in a God way!) and it had to spread! In the same way, when God first ignited a flame in your heart for Him and for His Gospel, it was always intended to burn like an inferno inside you, only getting bigger, hotter and brighter – burning in your heart and in your bones until the flames spill out and reach the people around you.

Perhaps that's why back in the 18th century when John Wesley was asked why people were coming from all over the place to hear him preach, his answer was: *"I set my self on fire and they come to watch me burn."*

Fire spreads.

**FUEL**

In countries where massive bushfires happen all the time (like Australia), fire-fighters have found a way of stopping the blaze in its tracks. It's called back-burning and it involves lighting smaller fires in the path of the wildfire, so that by the time the wildfire reaches that place, there's nothing left for it to feed on. It works because without fuel, even the biggest most ferocious fires soon burn out and die.

When it comes to living out the cross-driven mission, however, the challenge isn't how to quench the flames but how to keep them burning and spreading. We all know what it feels like to be fully on fire and in love with Jesus one minute and then stone-cold and struggling the next. Is it really possible to burn bright non-stop?

Yes.

Fire needs 2 things to survive: oxygen and fuel. Provided it's got both of those it'll burn forever. The Oxygen that we need as Christians is the power of the Holy Spirit in our lives. As far as the fuel goes, however – there's loads of different stuff that we can chuck into the furnace to feed the flames of the gospel, but it's really important to remember that it's not just *what* we do or *how* we do it that matters. God's also bothered about why we're doing it too.

Our motives matter!

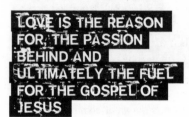

LOVE IS THE REASON FOR THE PASSION BEHIND AND ULTIMATELY THE FUEL FOR THE GOSPEL OF JESUS

You could write a ton of books on all the different things that should be motivating us to spread the word about Jesus, but it's actually easier to just sum it all up in one word:

Love!

Like we found out in chapter two, love is the reason for, the passion behind and ultimately the fuel for the Gospel of Jesus. If there's one energy-source that's enough on its own to keep us burning big and bright till the day we drop – then it's got to be love!

King Solomon said that *"[love] burns like blazing fire, like a mighty flame."* [111]

He was spot on!

Love is what took Christ all the way to the cross and beyond.

Love is why the cross-driven mission's still alive and kicking today.

Love is what should be firing us up and driving us out to spread the Word.

Here's why…

## MEGOS

There's a story in the Bible about a gang of Pharisees who were getting sick of people banging on about how fantastic Jesus was, so they confronted Him to try and trip Him up with their Bible skills. Unfortunately they just didn't understand that Jesus is the Son of God – the author and superstar of the same Scriptures that they were trying to catch Him out with. Duh!

(Mental note – don't bother trying to outsmart God. Ever. You'll always lose!)

Anyway, this is how it went down: One of them was an 'expert' in God's law (in other words he was a fast-talking, Slick-Rick with an Armani suit and a Mercedes camel) and

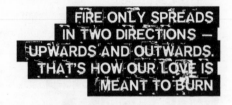

FIRE ONLY SPREADS IN TWO DIRECTIONS – UPWARDS AND OUTWARDS. THAT'S HOW OUR LOVE IS MEANT TO BURN

he asked Jesus this question: *"Teacher, which is the great commandment in the law?"* [112] Now the Greek word for 'great' is 'megos', which is where we get the word 'mega' from. So they were basically asking *"Jesus, what's the Mega Command?*

*The BIG one.*

*The one that matters most to God."*

As always, Jesus' reply was inspired:

*"'You must love the Lord your God with all your heart, all your soul, and all your mind.' This is the first and greatest commandment. A second is equally important: 'Love your neighbour as yourself.' The entire law and all the demands of the prophets are based on these two commandments."* [113]

What's mega important to God?

Love!

Loving Him with all that we've got, and loving others like we want to be loved.

Think of it like this: Fire only spreads in two directions – upwards and outwards. That's how our love is meant to burn – upwards to God in passionate worship and outwards to the world in compassionate witness.

## BURNING UP

**OUR LOVE FOR GOD SHOULD BE ENOUGH ON ITS OWN TO SEND US OUT.**

I find it so hard these days to walk the streets or watch the news, without being left broken-hearted, gutted, shocked or all of the above by what's going on! It's impossible not be moved by it, especially as a Christian who's now looking at the world through God's eyes. God loves the hurting people of our world deeply, and so should we. However, we need to be careful that loving the lost doesn't become our chief motive for the cross-driven mission, as John Stott reminds us:

*"The highest of missionary motives is neither obedience to the Great Commission (important as it is), not love for sinners who are alienated and perishing (strong as that incentive is, especially when we contemplate the wrath of God…), but rather zeal – burning and passionate zeal – for the glory of Jesus Christ."* [114]

Jesus was clear about what our first focus as missionaries should be – love that burns upwards in worship:

***"You must love the Lord your God with all your heart, all your soul, and all your mind. This is the first and greatest commandment."***

Now Jesus' mega command wasn't just about mission, it was a challenge to every single part of a Christian's life. That said, however, mission should always be part of what we're about as Christians, and our love for God should be enough on its own to send us out. It's like Matt Redman wrote:

*"Let worship be the fuel for mission's flame, we're going with a passion for Your Name."* [115]

# 1. Loving God For Who He Is

*"You must love the Lord..."*

When it comes to loving God, we really haven't got to look far to find reasons to love Him. Not just because of all the amazing stuff He's done (more about that later), but purely just because of who He is:

He's the infinite, immaculate, immortal King. He owns heaven. He's the most powerful being in existence. He's the supreme judge and ruler of all things. He's an all-consuming fire who's so magnificent that no one can look at Him and live. You can't get away from

**CHOOSING TO OBEY JESUS AND GO FOR IT WITH THE GOSPEL WILL REVEAL SOMETHING INCREDIBLE ABOUT YOU — THAT IT'S YOUR LOVE FOR THE LORD THAT FUELS YOUR FLAMES AND DRIVES YOU ON.**

Him because He's everywhere all the time. He had no beginning and will never end. He created everything and everyone in history. He knows the name of every star and has numbered every hair on every person's head ever. He's intimately concerned about all that goes on in His universe, which is just as well because He's the One who holds it all together. He's absolutely and entirely perfect in every way. He's the source of all light and all life. All true hope, peace, happiness and satisfaction come from Him. He never fails, never gives up and never breaks a promise. He invented grace. He IS love!

There really aren't enough words in any language to describe just how incredibly awesome He really is! The Pharisees, however, never realised that this Jesus, who was standing in front of them, was (and still is) that same LORD. If they had, they would have grasped that there's nothing and no one who deserved their love, worship and respect more than He does. Even the Old Testament Bible that they knew back-to-front said the same thing:

*"Love the LORD, all you His saints."* [116]

Do you love Him?

If you do, then remember that people will do anything for someone they love, so choosing to obey Jesus and go for it with the Gospel will reveal something incredible about you – that it's your love for the LORD that fuels your flames and drives you on. It's like Jesus said: *"If you love me, you will obey my commands."*[117]

# 2. Loving God For What He's Done

*"You must love…your God"*

OK, time for a little bit of honesty here – loving God doesn't always come easily to us. Quite the opposite in fact! The reality is that from the very moment that daddy's sperm got together with mummy's egg and said *"hey you're cute – let's get together and make a baby!"* sin kicked-in and we bungee-jumped into the world with a fist in God's face and a "stuff you God" attitude!

We're rebels from the start.

How then is it even possible for us to love Him as our God, if by nature we're His enemies?

The miracle is that Jesus' mega command is possible for us because a few chapters later Jesus went to the cross, smashed the sin barrier to bits and opened up a way for us to know God as our God. By doing that, He single-handedly transformed our status from enemy to family, or as the Bible puts it, *"[Jesus] made peace through the blood of His cross."* [118]

# OFFENSIVE 🔥

There's an amazing story in Luke 7 of a woman who was regarded as little more than a local whore by everyone in town, but who gate-crashed a party to pour a beautiful mixture of precious oil and tears of devotion all over Jesus' feet. Obviously everyone kicked-off about it because of her reputation, but Jesus saw straight through the pain and shame of her past and into a once-broken heart that had now been completely melted and mended by grace. Check out what He said:

*"I tell you, her sins—and they are many—have been forgiven, so she has shown me much love. But a person who is forgiven little shows only little love."* [119]

Because of her filthy past and the depth of grace that had made her clean, that woman understood more of God's love than anyone else in that room, and her response was to shamelessly bow down and wash the same feet that would soon be pierced by savage nails as He died for all her sin.

WHEN WE FULLY GET TO GRIPS WITH JUST HOW IMMENSE GOD'S LOVE FOR US REALLY IS, AND HOW FAR HE WAS WILLING TO GO TO PROVE IT – ALL WE CAN DO IS LOVE HIM BACK

Her response was worship!

When we fully get to grips with just how immense God's love for us really is, and how far He was willing to go to prove it – all we can do is love Him back. Here's how one of Jesus best mates (John) puts it:

*"We love Him because He first loved us."* [120]

When my daughter Elen was just 6 months old, she was rushed into hospital after suffering a febrile convulsion (temperature-related fit). She was kept in for three days as doctors battled to stabilise her temperature, and it was one of the most upsetting things I've ever been through – helplessly looking on as my little girl, complete with IV drip in her tiny arm, lay there shivering, shaking and scared.

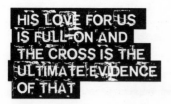

HIS LOVE FOR US
IS FULL-ON AND
THE CROSS IS THE
ULTIMATE EVIDENCE
OF THAT

It was in this traumatic setting that God revealed something to me about His love that transformed my understanding of the cross for ever. I was making a coffee in the parents' room and chatting with the dad of another child who was sick, when I made the comment that *"I'd do anything to swap places with my little girl right now!"* And I honestly would have. I can't describe how deeply I love my daughter. It's not a feeling I'd ever experienced before becoming a dad, and it's not something I can adequately put into words. I just really, really, really, really, really, really, really love her! If I could have been infected with her sickness, while she went home healthy and whole – I would have done it like a shot! Any father worth his salt would! And that's when the penny dropped! Father God saw the tragedy of our world, packed to the rafters with children He loves, whose lives had been trashed by sin and death, and who were hurtling towards an eternity without Him, and His loving response was: *"I'd do anything to swap places with them!"*

So that's exactly what He did!

Our God loves us more passionately, more permanently and more powerfully than we'll ever fully understand. How can we not love Him back? His love for us is full-on and the cross is the ultimate evidence of that. That's why our mission is cross-driven, because the cross both saves us and inspires us! It proves God's love to us and sends us out with love in our hearts.

And people will do anything for someone they love.

If loving God is the ultimate fuel for the flames of mission, then let's never, ever, ever take our eyes off the cross of love!

# 3. Loving God With All We've Got

*"You must love...with all your heart, with all your soul, and with all your mind."*

WE NEED TO LOVE GOD WITH ABSOLUTELY EVERYTHING!!!

Love is such an over-used word that it's kind of lost it's meaning these days!

*"I love chocolate."*

*"I love my wife."*

Now if I really loved chocolate like I love my wife then I might as well have married a mars-bar! OK, that's obviously stupid, but the mega-love that Jesus was on about needs to go so much deeper than our love for food, fashion, or even our families!

We need to love God with absolutely everything!!!

When you set fire to a lump of wood, it'll burn and burn until there's nothing left to give. That's how fuel works. You won't find a piece of wood that jumps out of the fire shouting *"Right, I've had enough. I'm feeling burnt-out and unappreciated so I'm giving up!"* Wood will literally burn itself to death – going out in a blaze of glory!

Our worship needs to be like that!

We need to love God with all our heart, soul, mind and strength. If we could just fully love God in these four areas, our love for Him would seriously start to blaze like wildfire and our world would soon start to feel the heat!

# HEART

IF YOU'RE GOING TO LOVE GOD FROM THE HEART, YOU NEED TO GIVE HIM ALL OF IT!

Every year on Valentine's Day (a.k.a National Puke Fest) gangs of soppy teenagers play their part in destroying entire rain-forests (and thereby killing the planet) by sending lorry loads of sickly valentines cards to each other. They've normally got a little ♥ on there somewhere, because love has apparently got something to do with it all, and love is all about the heart. But when Jesus says that we should be loving God with all out heart, He's not talking about the fluffy, sugary, neon pink, kiss-me-quick sort of love that hormone-crazed teenagers are after.

Heart-love is so much deeper than all that!

When the Bible talks about the heart it literally means the very core of a person. It's the place where passion and emotion and purpose and belief and attitude and appetite and drive and desire and courage come from. Your heart forms the very fabric of who you are and what you're all about. It's the real you.

Who/what are you passionate about?

Who/what drives you?

Who/what gets you out of bed in the mornings?

Who/what are you living for?

The answer to these questions will reveal the truth about your heart right now, and where you're at with Jesus' mega command. If you're going to love God from the heart, you need to give Him all of it! Don't hold anything back – it's all or nothing! He should be the absolute focus of your life. His mission should be your passion and His purposes should be your priority. His desires should drive you on, and His cross should give you courage.

When you devote your whole heart to loving God, His fire will start burning hotter inside you and will soon burst its way out into the lives of those around you.

**OFFENSIVE**

Your heart will change.

Your life will change.

Your world will change.

If you really want to feed the flames of cross-driven mission – love your God with all your heart!

## SOUL

You are not just a monkey holding a book!

One of the amazing things about faith in God
is the dignity of not having to believe the lie that you're just a cosmic accident whose not so distant relatives include chimpanzees, sludge, and various explosive gases! The Bible's crystal clear that you were intelligently and lovingly designed by God, and that your status as a human being sets you apart from everything else that He has made. That makes you special!

*"Then the Lord God formed the man from the dust of the ground. He breathed the breath of life into the man's nostrils, and the man became a living person"* [121]

That breath is what makes us special.

God didn't just breath physical life into Adam's schnozzle back in Eden but He also breathed spiritual life into him too, making him an eternal, spiritual being. In other words – Adam got soul, and so do we!

Jesus said that we should love God with all our soul. The Greek word for soul is 'psuche' which can mean the breath of life or the part of the body that isn't destroyed by death. So we need to be loving God with every breath that we take! Our soul is the spiritual part of us that will last forever, and although our sin problem means that we're all born spiritually dead and destined for eternal hell, the resurrection life that Jesus dishes out has jump-started our spirituality, put us on the road to heaven and made it possible for us to love God *"in spirit and truth."* [122]

So then, is your spiritual life ruled by your love for God? Do you love Him enough to spend time with Him every day praying and getting stuck into His Word? Are you sold-out for the One who saved your soul? Do you love Him enough to not just relax until you get your Jacuzzi in heaven, but to live every day like you're grateful to be going there at all?!

If you are then be encouraged, because a soul-soaked with passion for Jesus guarantees that while you're loving Him and living His mission – there's no such thing as a wasted breath.

## MIND

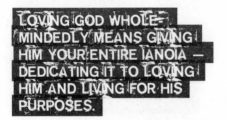
LOVING GOD WHOLE-MINDEDLY MEANS GIVING HIM YOUR ENTIRE IANOIA – DEDICATING IT TO LOVING HIM AND LIVING FOR HIS PURPOSES.

Your mind is a seriously powerful bit of kit!

Apparently most of us think at a rate of around 10 thoughts per second (while we're awake). That's like 36,000 thoughts per hour. 604,800 thoughts per day. 114,847,771,860,000,000 thoughts per average lifetime! That's a lot of brain-activity!

Now some thoughts are almost sub-conscious like: breathe, blink, burp! Others are just general decision-making ones like: Shall I get out of bed? Shall I change my pants this week? Why did I just get out of bed? However, there's also a whole load of other stuff that goes on inside your melon that's much, much deeper than all that stuff!

Mahatma Gandhi (famous Indian chap) once said that: *"A man is but the product of his thoughts. What he thinks, he becomes."*

If that's true, then what would your thought-life turn you into?

A workaholic? A stress-head? A sex-machine? A worshipper?

In the Bible the Greek word for 'mind' is 'ianoia' which can be translated as our way of thinking and feeling, or our thought-life (good and bad). And Jesus has

# OFFENSIVE

commanded us to love God with all of it! That's a serious challenge to people like us who's heads soon get filled-up with all sorts of random rubbish and selfishness. Loving God whole-mindedly means giving Him your entire ianoia – dedicating it to loving Him and living for His purposes. It means using your God-given gifts, skills, creativity and ambition for Him, all in the name of putting a smile on His face and cracking on with His mission.

I guess you could call it being mental for Jesus.

## STRENGTH

We've already seen that loving God with all we've got requires every ounce of our emotional, spiritual and mental passion. However, if we're going to literally love Him with absolutely everything, there's still one final area of our lives that we need to

EVERY LAST DROP OF OUR 'ISCHUS ENERGY' WAS ONLY EVER GIVEN TO US SO THAT WE COULD EMPTY IT ALL STRAIGHT BACK OUT FOR GOD AND FOR HIS GLORY

lay down. We can find it in Mark's account of the 'mega-command' story: *"You must love the LORD your God with... all your strength."* [123] The Greek word for strength here is 'ischus' which means force, strength, or might. That means that if we're going to love our God to the max – we need to get used to the idea that it's going to be sweaty!

Are you loving God with all your strength? Not some of it, or even most of it but all of it?

GOD WANTS US TO LOVE HIM WITH EVERY FIBRE OF WHO WE ARE – HEART AND SOUL, BRAINS AND BRAWN!

Do you live and move and work and play as your worship to God?

Is it your pure love for Him that gives you the strength to carry on when you've had enough and feel like quitting?

The truth is that when it comes to loving God, there's simply no room for selfishness in this area! In an age when people are spending more time, money and effort on health, wealth and personal pampering, than on praising God and living for Him, it's crucial that we remember that every last drop of our 'ischus energy' was only ever given to us so that we could empty it all straight back out for God and for His glory.

God wants us to love Him with every fibre of who we are – heart and soul, brains and brawn! If that sounds harsh then, then we need to take a fresh look at Skull Hill, where God's Son poured out every last drop of His passion for us on the cross. He gave more of Himself emotionally, mentally, physically and above all spiritually, than we ever could.

He did it for us.

He did it in the name of love!

What better motive do we need?

## BURNING OUT

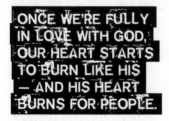

ONCE WE'RE FULLY IN LOVE WITH GOD, OUR HEART STARTS TO BURN LIKE HIS – AND HIS HEART BURNS FOR PEOPLE.

When I first met my wife we were very different. I was a mouthy, tattooed drum & bass DJ with an attitude problem, who spent a lot more time on a skateboard than attending to personal hygiene! She was gentle, beautiful, godly, beautiful, freakishly intelligent, caring, beautiful and really into acoustic rock! Love at first sight it wasn't!!! Anyway, God decided that I needed a fresh dollop of grace in my life, and that Michelle needed a *real* challenge, so He made us fall in love, get married, get a dog and start a family! We both loved Jesus though, so at least the foundations were all there.

Now, if I was to say that as soon as we'd said the words *"I do"*, that I was overwhelmed with a desire to start washing every day, or that she was overcome with an urge to gradually deafen herself with dark and swirly bass-lines I'd be lying! But we have changed! I genuinely do appreciate acoustic guitars and have even written the odd song. I also smell better! She now loves funky drum & bass, eats curry and doesn't feel the need to hide behind make-up every day!

The thing is, when you love someone – you change! Their passions become your passions! Their ways become your ways. Their heart becomes your heart! That's why loving the lost is part two of Jesus' mega command, because once we're fully in love with God, our heart starts to burn like His – and His heart burns for people.

# 4. Loving Others Because God Does

*"Love your neighbour..."*

Because I grew up in the 80's, it's impossible to hear Jesus talking about neighbours, without thinking about the tangled love-lives of the heavily mulleted Australian pop-stars of Ramsay Street (surely the most dangerous cul-de-sac in the world). Anyway, the good news is that Jesus' command to love our neighbours had

WE NEED TO PEOPLE WHO ARE PASSIONATE ABOUT PEOPLE. WHY? BECAUSE GOD LOVES PEOPLE – THE GOOD, THE BAD, AND THE DOWNRIGHT DISGUSTING!

absolutely nothing to do with mullets, music or chucking some more shrimps on the barby!

He was actually quoting Leviticus 19v18 (part of the Jewish Old Testament) in which the Hebrew word for 'neighbour' is 'Rea', which can mean 'friend', 'companion' or 'any other fellow human-being!' Jesus was saying that we need to be people who love those we're close to (friends and family), those we rub shoulders with every day (colleagues, community people etc.) and anyone else with a beating heart and breath in their lungs (the rest of humanity!)

One of Jesus' disciples called James (a.k.a 'son of thunder') called this command the 'Royal Law', and said that if we live by it then we're *"doing well."*[124] So what does it mean to love our neighbour? I guess it means that we need to be people who are passionate about people. Why? Because God loves people – the good, the bad, and the downright disgusting! Check out what God said to Jonah back in the O.T about the wicked and wild city of Nineveh: **"And should I not pity Nineveh, that great city, in which there are more than 120,000 persons who do not know their right hand from their left, and also much cattle?"**[125] You've got to love the fact that God was bothered about the cows too, but it was blatantly the lost people of Nineveh who His heart was really burning for!

The gospel is God's love story to the world.

If you want to see just how much God loves people, look no further than Jesus. His mission statement (Luke 4v18-19) made it clear what He was all about – He came for the poor, the imprisoned, the blind and the beaten. It was His compassion that led Him to reach, touch and transform the baddest and most broken people in town. The tears that he shed over the city of Jerusalem flowed from the depths of His love for people who were dangerously lost like sheep without a shepherd. If we're going to love our neighbour the Jesus-way, we need a piece of that compassion too:

We need to love our families – busy husbands, tired wives, psychotic brothers, emotional sisters, hilarious grandparents, embarrassing aunties and disobedient dogs – because God does!

We need to love our communities – noisy neighbours, stressed-out schoolmates, hassled shoppers, and even the little ASBO crew down the end of the street who smash stuff up – because God does!

We need to love the world – the hurting and homeless, the used and abused, the addicted and afflicted, the down-trodden and messed-up, the war-torn and the weeping, the starving and the struggling – because God does!

We need to love our enemies – the God-haters, the religious hypocrites, the ones who mock us, threaten us, attack us or even try to take our lives from us – because God does! That's who Jesus loved, and the flames of His outrageous compassion for people have never died down since!
He wants us to burn like that too.

# OFFENSIVE 🔥

Erwin MacManus said it this way:

*"Jesus came to ignite a fire within you that would consume you and ignite you. Jesus the King came to fight for your heart. If He has won your heart, then to follow your heart will always lead you to advance forward behind enemy lines to win the hearts of those who do not yet know Him or love Him."* [126]

# 5. Loving Others Like God Does

*"Love your neighbour as yourself."*

One time, Jesus was approached by a different 'expert' in God's law, to chat about God's mega command. He

SELFLESS LOVE IS AN IRRESISTIBLE FORCE.

asked Jesus to clarify exactly *who* our neighbour is. Jesus answered him by telling him the story of a bloke who was travelling to Jericho when he got jumped by a bunch of thugs who robbed him, beat him up and left him for dead. Two religious leaders from his neighbourhood saw him lying in the gutter covered in blood, and each took one look at how messed-up he was and crossed the road to avoid getting their hands dirty.

But then something sensational happened.

A bloke from a rival community saw him, and rather than sticking the boot in, his heart was stirred with compassion and he crossed the road to help him. He bandaged his wounds up, gave him a free ride on his donkey to a local pub and paid for him to stay and recuperate out of his own pocket, with a promise of more cash if it was needed!

Jesus asked the curious lawyer, who he thought was a neighbour in the true sense of the word. The lawyer rightly replied *"the one who showed him mercy."*[127]

Jesus doesn't just want us to love our neighbour. He wants us to love our neighbour as ourselves, and that's not as easy or comfortable as it sounds. The good neighbour in Jesus' story had absolutely no reason to show love to the guy who'd had his head kicked in. He loved because he wanted to, even though it cost him. What really gets me is there's not even a mention of gratitude, or whether he even got a 'thank you!'

That's grace in action.

Some people have said that showing grace like that is just opening yourself up to be a doormat for people to walk all over. As far as I'm concerned, however, as long as I'm a doormat that says 'Welcome to heaven' people can trample over me all they want because selfless love is an irresistible force.

Ask yourself this one simple question: If you spent as much time thinking about, spending money on, praying for and taking care of others as you did for yourself, what would your life look like? Think hard about that, because the answer will paint an accurate picture of the quality of your love for others.

The truth is that Jesus' command to love others like we love ourselves goes completely against our human nature, because we're just not wired that way! But if that's the fuel we need for the cross-driven mission, we'd best get serious about it! Again, a glimpse into the pure life of Jesus shows us all we need to see of selfless love in action – a Teacher who was tired, but decided that feeding 5000 hungry followers was more important than rest. A man who sweat blood in the shadow of the cross, but still prayed *"not My will, but Yours be done."* [128] A Saviour who was nailed unjustly and violently to a cross, yet chose not to call down a legion of heavyweight angels to give His enemies a kicking, but rather chose to stick it out and win salvation and eternal life for them instead!

That's 'others-first' love!

That's what our world needs to see in us. There's an awesome chunk of Bible that lays out what selfless, God-style love is like. Read it through. Pray it through. And ask God to ignite that kind of love in your life:

# OFFENSIVE ↻

*"Love never gives up.*
*Love cares more for others than for self.*
*Love doesn't want what it doesn't have.*
*Love doesn't strut,*
*Doesn't have a swelled head,*
*Doesn't force itself on others, isn't always "me first,"*
*Doesn't fly off the handle,*
*Doesn't keep score of the sins of others,*
*Doesn't revel when others grovel,*
*Takes pleasure in the flowering of truth,*
*Puts up with anything,*
*Trusts God always,*
*Always looks for the best,*
*Never looks back,*
*But keeps going to the end.*
*Love never dies."* [129]

That's life-touching, deep-reaching, world-changing love! That's what the people all around you need a taste of. Have you got fire like that blazing in your heart and burning through your bones?

Me neither!

But I want it so bad. I want God to make me that person! There's no greater fuel for the cross-driven mission than full-on, sold-out, no-holding-back love for God and for the people He died for!

**THERE'S NO GREATER FUEL FOR THE CROSS-DRIVEN MISSION THAN FULL-ON, SOLD-OUT, NO-HOLDING-BACK LOVE FOR GOD AND FOR THE PEOPLE HE DIED FOR!**

Set me on fire LORD.

Set *us* on fire – and send us out to burn for you!

# THE AFTERMATH

# BECCI'S STORY

> How has the love of Christ impacted my life?

Love never fails. The truth of those words resonates throughout the Bible. The message of the cross shows us God's great love, displayed for all to see, and his victory over death and his resurrection proves that God's promises never fail.

Just as we see the love of God on the cross, so we are called to reflect it to our generation. The Father heart of God for this broken generation before us is exploding into the passions of young people across the world, just as it did to me during the Offensive course.

The overwhelming greatness of God's presence has impacted my life forever changing my thoughts and transforming my life. Offensive not only showed me the grace and love of God through the teaching, worship and ministry but also through the love of the fellowship and family that surrounded me throughout the course. The love of Christ for transforming this generation and this world shone from them, and their passion was infectious.

Reflecting Christ's love for the world seems relatively easy in the company of other Christians, but in today's world, that seems so lacking in love, we are called to be lights in the darkness, witnesses of Christ's love in our everyday lives. The impact of the love of God has utterly transformed my world. I have been saved by His amazing grace why wouldn't I want everyone else to experience it too.

We love because God first loved us.

# CHAPTER FIVE

## RIGHTEOUS REVOLUTION

"NOW IS THE TIME FOR US TO SHINE." [130]

- DELIRIOUS?

# OFFENSIVE

## REVOLUTION

I don't want to sound like ASBO material, but I need to confess that I'm a big fan of graffiti. You know the colourful, creative urban art (that requires skill), not the 'shazza lvz dazza 4 eva' stuff (that requires stupidity). My appreciation of street writing means that I always look twice at any wall with a mural or a message on it, because I truly am fascinated by aerosol art. Anyway, I was recently on my way into the centre of Cardiff when I walked past a wall that had the following words sprayed on it: *"In a world full of deceit the truth is a revolutionary act."* It really got me thinking. In an age when corruption and unfaithfulness are rife, truth really is revolutionary! And then I really got excited, because Jesus said that He is the truth [131], which I guess makes Him a revolutionary. That's cool!

The more I look at Jesus' life, the more I get it – Jesus never came to start a religion – He came to ignite a revolution of faith, hope and love that would change the world forever. Right at the start of His whole gospel adventure, Jesus went to the synagogue, grabbed a copy of the book of Isaiah and read out what was essentially His mission-statement:

*"The Spirit of the LORD is upon me,*
*Because He has anointed me*
*To preach the gospel to the poor;*
*He has sent me to heal the broken-*
*hearted,*
*To proclaim liberty to the captives*
*And recovery of sight to the blind,*
*To set at liberty those who are oppressed;*
*To proclaim the acceptable year of the LORD."* [132]

JESUS NEVER CAME TO START A RELIGION — HE CAME TO IGNITE A REVOLUTION OF FAITH, HOPE AND LOVE THAT WOULD CHANGE THE WORLD FOREVER

That's revolutionary living! I love how no one could accuse Jesus of being all talk – His life of grace was as revolutionary as the gospel on His lips, and everywhere He went the revolution spread! The poor, the broken-hearted, the blind, the cast-down and the chained-up – they all heard the Gospel preached by the way that that Jesus lived, as well as by the words that He spoke. And what really blesses my little cotton socks off is that He's called us to join the revolution too, proclaiming the gospel with our voices and backing it up with our lives. Confronting the powers of darkness that are trashing the world He loves, and laying down our lives for the righteous cause of seeing heaven come on earth.

That's revolution Jesus-style.

## TASTE & SEE

**IF THEY WON'T LISTEN TO THE GOOD NEWS, WE JUST NEED TO SHOW THEM THE GOOD NEWS**

One of the most heart-breaking things that we face on the cross-driven mission is the tragic reality that many people (for all sorts of reasons) simply don't want to know the beautiful message of God's love and salvation. They don't want to hear about Jesus, don't care that He died for them, don't believe that He's alive and don't want to listen to anyone banging on about the old, old story of the gospel. The bible's clear, however, that the only way that they'll get to heaven is if they're saved by faith [133], and faith only come by hearing the gospel. [134]

So where does that leave us? We can't exactly kidnap people, zip-tie them to a chair in a dark basement, force them to listen to what we've got to say and tell them that the only way they'll ever see the light of day again is if they pray the sinner's prayer (and really mean it in their hearts!) That kind of evangelism's not generally advisable (unless you want to try your hand at prison ministry for 10+ years!) So I suppose if they won't listen to the good news, we just need to show them the good news. To live radical cross-driven, good news lives that both build bridges for the gospel, and back-up our message too, giving it credibility in a sceptical world.

In one of His many famous songs, King David wrote **"taste and see that the LORD is good."** [135] They're powerful lyrics that challenge the listener – if you won't listen to the gospel, then why don't you come and experience it for yourself. I don't know about you, but that's what I want for my generation. I want them to taste and see that my God – the real, living God – isn't the One associated with all the terrorism, hatred, hypocrisy and oppression done in His name that causes people to hate the very idea of God. But rather He's a good God, a compassionate God who loves them, weeps for them and died to save them.

However, seeing as there's no 'God Shops' in town where people can pop in and ask for a suck-it-and-see sample of God's goodness, where can people go?

Jesus' solution was revolutionary – to saturate the world with an army of 'ordinary radicals'[136] who function as buckets of pure salt and shafts of irresistible light in a dark and dirty world:

*"You are the salt of the earth…You are the light of the world. A city set on a hill cannot be hidden. Nor do people light a lamp and put it under a basket, but on a stand and it gives light to all in the house. In the same way, let your light shine before others, so that they may see your good works and give glory to your Father who is in heaven."* [137]

Nothing enhances flavour like salt, and nothing illuminates the darkness like light. Jesus has called us to be both.

# 1. Salty

*"You are the salt of the earth…"*

Salt had several uses back in Jesus' day.

First up, salt was used in exactly the same way as it is today – sprinkly, sprinkly on bags of chips (or whatever else they were eating back then!) Now I never realized just how much flavour salt gives to food until my little girl started eating proper food with us, so we had to start cooking meals with zero salt. Uuugggghhh! Salt-less food is just rank – bland, tasteless and…boring!

Something that I hear time and time again from youth that I spend time with on the streets is that they're bored. How can anyone in this generation be bored? There are more sports facilities, skateparks and shops than ever before. We've got hi-tech gizmos like i-Pods, mobiles and lap-tops, hi-speed internet connections, DVDs and widescreen TVs bursting out of our ears – how can anyone be bored? There are kids the same age, but living in abject poverty in Africa, Asia and Latin America, who get hours of pleasure simply by kicking a rag-football round in the mud all day. How can anyone from our ends ever claim to be bored?

The way I see it is people aren't bored at all – they're just deeply unsatisfied!

It's like pigging out on junk-food might be nice for a treat and it may fill you up for a little while, but if you made it your daily diet, it wouldn't be long until your system started kicking off because it was lacking all the nutrients and stuff that it needed to healthy and strong. Meat and veg might not always be top of our favourites list, but it's the kind of stuff that we need if we don't want to get ill. Our generation, perhaps more than any other in history, has been frantically stuffing its face on junk like casual sex, binge drinking, drug experimentation, and the pursuit of wealth for so long now, that it's little wonder that people are starting to get sick.

When salt is put on food it does two things. It enhances the taste and it makes you thirsty. When Jesus told us that we're to live like salt, He was telling us that our lives of faith, hope and love are meant to taste so good to others that they start getting hungry for it themselves. It's like have you ever walked past a restaurant (or even a kebab house) with an empty gut, and got a whiff of what they're cooking? It's like *"Oh my days – I've just got to have some of that!"* The challenge of the cross-driven life is to live in such a radically different way to everyone else, that people who are sick of the world's junk and hungry for true satisfaction, get a whiff of what Jesus is doing in our lives, and cry out *"Oh my days – I've just got to have some of that!"*

Another effect of salt is that it creates thirst.

I love the story of the time when Jesus broke all cultural, social and religious barriers to speak with a shady lady at a watering hole in Samaria. After asking her for a drink, Jesus said to her: ***"Everyone who drinks of this water will be thirsty again, but whoever drinks of the water that I will give him will never be thirsty forever. The water that I will give him will become in him a spring of water welling up to eternal life."*** [138]

Not only was this woman physically thirsty (it was midday in a hot country), she was also spiritually thirsty. Her track record of failed marriages, shattered dreams, and a broken heart had left her clamming for healing, wholeness and a fresh start. The promise of living water that could cleanse and revive her, flooding her life with the abundance of God, was more than she could resist. After Jesus had gently helped her recognize her need of

**THE CHALLENGE TO US IS TO LIVE REVOLUTIONARY LIVES THAT ARE SO GOD-FLAVOURED AND SALTY THAT THEY CAUSE THOSE WHO ARE GASPING FOR TRUE LIFE TO TURN TO JESUS**

a Saviour, and then revealed to her that He was that Saviour, she left her water jar at the well, returned to her town, and sparked a mini-revival as the living water of Jesus flowed through her in to the lives of others.

All around us on the streets, buses, in schools, homes, shops and communities, people are thirsting like never before for the soul-quenching, life-giving water of the gospel. The challenge to us is to live revolutionary lives that are so God-flavoured and salty that they cause those who are gasping for true life to turn to Jesus for what they need. After all, it was Him who said:

*"Blessed are those who hunger and thirst for righteousness, for they shall be satisfied."* [139]

# 2. Authentic

There's another thing that salt was used for back in Bible times that's much less familiar to us, and it's all about poo! (Now seeing as my name's Mr. Hankey – I really do find writing about poo quite ironic!!! [140]) Anyway, back in Bible times they didn't have flushing toilets and sewers, so if you needed to do a number two, you'd have to dispose of your doo-doo by chucking it on a dung-hill.

And dung-hills aren't pleasant places, as I've personally experienced.

When my dog Boaz was a puppy I used to scoop up his poo from the back yard and put it in a little pile in the corner of the garden (we called it 'Cac Corner!)

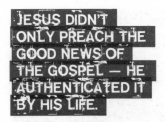

JESUS DIDN'T ONLY PREACH THE GOOD NEWS OF THE GOSPEL — HE AUTHENTICATED IT BY HIS LIFE.

Anyway, that little pile eventually became a small mountain, and by the time I had to move house, it filled 2 black bin-bags! Despite having a peg on my nose and holding my breath for as long as possible – I couldn't just smell it, I could literally taste it as I shovelled it into the bags, my eyes streaming with water! Poo stinks and it also spreads disease, so you can imagine what the dung-hill for an entire town would have been like. Nasty! The way that they used to combat the stench and risk of disease was by shovelling a load of salt all over the steaming heap! The salt would filter out the impurities and stop the filth spreading any further.

The gospels are packed with stories of Jesus confronting poverty, injustice, greed, hypocrisy, and sin in general – trampling on whatever was evil, wicked and deathly, and powerfully demonstrating the righteousness and glory of God against all odds. That's revolutionary. That's being salt in a dirty world. I love that Jesus didn't only preach the good news of the Gospel – He authenticated it by His life.

Christians are often criticized for being so heavenly minded that they're of no earthly use, which is gutting because that's the exact opposite of what Jesus was getting at when He called us the salt of the earth. We're called to be slap-bang in the middle of all the poo, actively standing against the spread of the sin that's staining our world. That might involve us doing big stuff like campaigning for issues of global justice (such as people trafficking, AIDS, Fair Trade etc.), sponsoring children out of poverty through Christian agencies like Compassion[141], or finding ways to feed and clothe the homeless. Or it could mean engaging the world in smaller, more personal ways like comforting someone when they're crying, being a friend to someone who's got none, opposing bullies or spending time with lonely people.

Authenticating the gospel through social action is playing an increasingly prominent role in the cross-driven mission, and building significant bridges for proclaiming the gospel to a world that doesn't want to listen. Painting fences, rebuilding playgrounds, picking up some shopping for dear old Gladys…more and more

# OFFENSIVE

people (especially youth) are getting stuck in to their communities and exploring creative ways of demonstrating the good news of Jesus! While we must never

**SOCIAL ACTION IS PLAYING AN INCREASINGLY PROMINENT ROLE IN THE CROSS-DRIVEN MISSION, AND BUILDING SIGNIFICANT BRIDGES FOR PROCLAIMING THE GOSPEL TO A WORLD THAT DOESN'T WANT TO LISTEN.**

fall into the trap of *only* doing social action, I can't think of many better ways of illustrating what Jesus has done than stepping into a messy situation and getting our hands dirty as we pick up a whole load of filthy, stinking rubbish (that's not even our responsibility), sticking it in a sack, and taking it to the tip – never to be seen again. For free! That's the cross of Jesus right there!

Jesus has called us to be salty people who by our very nature make others hunger and thirst for all He has to offer. He encourages us to authenticate the gospel by the way we live, taking a revolutionary stand against the surge of sin in our world, and finding new and innovative ways of showing people what Jesus is really all about.

I saw just how powerful the combination of both living and speaking the gospel can be during the 2007 Summer Offensive (a week of focussed mission that we do off the back of running the Offensive course in Cardiff). I'd given the small team of hyped-up cross-driven missionaries the challenge of 'Your city. Your mission.' Allowing them the freedom to decide how they wanted to take the righteous revolution of Jesus to the streets of Cardiff (I was involved only in ensuring that none of their ideas were dangerous, illegal or heretical!). After a day of praying around the city, they came back and said *"There's so many homeless guys out there. We need to give them something to eat."*

So the next day they bought a bunch of food (with their own cash) made about forty packed lunches and took to the streets with bags full of food, and pockets stuffed with gospel flyers. Because of my arthritic skater's ankles, I literally couldn't keep up with them so every homeless person I tried blessing with some tucker had already been fed by the time I got there. I was getting a bit vexed when I saw something that stirred my heart so deeply I almost cried. Sat in a shop doorway was a homeless guy munching on a cheese sandwich with one hand, and reading a leaflet about the love of Jesus in the other!

Later in the week that same guy stopped and listened as the team did a gospel presentation in the centre of town. He approached some of the boys at the end and told them that he was hooked on heroin but wanted what they had. They were able to talk further with him about the gospel and pray with him before heading off.

That's authentic Christianity.

That's cross-driven living!

# 3. Identity

*"You are the light of the world..."*

My first ever car was a beige Mini estate called 'Maxwell'. He was a seriously fun little car, though he did have one or two quirky little problems. For example the choke only worked with a clothes peg on it, the fuel gauge didn't work at all and the back windows were only held in place by moss! Furthermore, the accelerator broke once, and the only way it got fixed was when my mate snapped a biro in half, taped the two halves together and shoved it somewhere up behind the pedals (to this day I don't know how or why it worked – it just did!) However, there was also a slightly more serious problem with Maxwell. Every once in a while, and with absolutely no warning, the headlights (and dashboard lights) would switch off. To get them to work again you had to switch them off and on again, which was fine if you could find the button (down by your knees somewhere).

Anyway, I was never really that bothered about the headlight thing until the time when I was traveling from Aberystwyth to Cardiff over the hills of mid-Wales in the middle of the night. Now anyone who knows anything about that stretch of road will no doubt be aware that it's a bit ropey to say the least. Not only are there gangs of ninja sheep with a death-wish that love jumping out of the shadows in front of you, but the roads are more twisty and turny than politicians at election time! Most dangerous of all, however, is the total absence of electricity in mid-Wales, meaning there's no street lighting for about 60 miles – a problem I became acutely aware

**THE WORLD NEEDS LIGHT, WHICH IS WHY THE GOAL OF THE CROSS-DRIVEN MISSION IS TO INTRODUCE PEOPLE TO JESUS "THE LIGHT OF THE WORLD."**

of at around 2am when Maxwell decided it was practical joke time. It was as I was heading towards a sharp hair-pin bend at about 60mph when it all went dark. VERY DARK!!! I literally couldn't see a thing as I slammed on the brakes and fumbled round my knees for the light switch, whilst doing everything in my control to hold my bladder! Because God's gracious (and no kamikaze sheep decided to get involved) I somehow survived. However, I realized that night just how scary the darkness can be, and how precious light is.

Now you probably don't need much convincing that our world's in darkness. Deep, dangerous darkness. It breaks my heart to see an entire generation of young people who should be loving life and living it to the max, but who instead lead an empty existence, stumbling from one calamity to the next, robbed of hope and crippled by fear: *"The way of the wicked is like deep darkness. They do not know what makes them stumble."* [142] Why do so many seem to be lost in darkness? Without being too scientific, it's because darkness is merely the absence of light, and because *"God is light"*[143], when people reject Him, they're essentially rejecting the light. The ultimate tragedy is that for those without the gospel, this life is as bright as it's going to get, as the darkness waiting for them beyond death is the eternal reality of the absence of God. That's a terrifying thought.

The world needs light, which is why the goal of the cross-driven mission is to introduce people to Jesus *"the light of the world."* [144] However, one of the mysteries of God that just pickles my noggin, is that we're not only called to point people to the light of the world, but Jesus Himself tells us that we *are* the light of the world! The only way that I can even begin to try and explain that is by encouraging you to look up and learn some lessons from the sun and the moon.

**WE ARE NOW IN HIM (BY FAITH),
HE'S NOW IN US (BY HIS SPIRIT)
AND ALL OF A SUDDEN WE
BECOME AGENTS OF CHANGE**

The sun is a massive ball of burning energy that lives about 94 million miles away from earth. It's surface burns at a mere 9,900°F, while the core can get as hot as 22.5 million°F. Even though it's so far away, it's perfectly placed to provide earth with all the heat, light and energy that we need to survive. The moon on the other hand is just a lump of stone cold rock, hundreds of times smaller than the sun, completely dead, and capable of creating no energy or supporting any life. However, purely by reflecting the light of the sun (kind of like a big mirror), the moon can illuminate the darkest night sky.

In a similar way, we're just like a bunch of tiny rocks who can do nothing to change this world on our own. However, when we let Jesus into our lives and dedicate ourselves to His mission and His purposes for us, we take on a brand-new identity in Him. We are now *in* Him (by faith), He's now *in* us (by His Spirit) and all of a sudden we become agents of change – an army of little lights reflecting the pure light of Jesus in the midst of the darkness.

We literally become the light of the world – and that's just intense.

# 4. Purpose

*"A city set on a hill cannot be hidden..."*

I live on a council estate called Trevethin that stands at 800ft above sea level in the South Wales valleys. It's great if you like gale force winds, don't get vertigo and can cope with altitude sickness. What I love about my 'city on a hill' though, is that you can see it from miles away (you can literally see it from the English side of the Bristol Channel). At night-time when all the street and house lights are on it becomes especially visible, shining bright on top of the hill for everyone to see. Christmas time's always the best because you get the added bonus of several hundred Las Vegas-style neon Santas twitching away into the night sky too.

# OFFENSIVE

Since living where I do, I've understood so much better what Jesus was trying to communicate when He called us a city on a hill. Cities aren't merely a network of streets, buildings, shops and

THERE ARE NO ACCIDENTAL HEROES ON THE CROSS-DRIVEN MISSION – WE WERE RESCUED FOR A REASON

parks. If they were – they'd be lifeless! If no one lived in Trevethin the place would be completely dead and invisible in the dark. Cities are made up of people. All sorts of people from various races and places, at different ages and stages of life, with a unique spectrum of gifts, skills, dreams and stories to tell.

It's people who light up cities.

In the same way, Jesus never saved us to stand alone. He's building a heavenly kingdom (a.k.a *"Zion, the perfection of beauty"* [145]) out of which *"God shines in glorious radiance."* [146] Sounds sweet doesn't it? Well check it out, He's hand-picked us to be part of it:

*"But you are a chosen race, a royal priesthood, a holy nation, a people for His own possession, that you may proclaim the excellencies of Him who called you out of darkness into marvellous light."* [147]

No city is ever built by accident, especially when it's high on top of a hill. Cities are built with a specific purpose in mind, and built at the expense of blood, sweat and tears. Jesus gave an abundance of all those on the cross as He paid what as necessary to make us part of His heavenly plan. There are no accidental heroes on the cross-driven mission – we were rescued for a reason. But exactly what purpose did He have in mind for us?

We were saved to shine – like a city on a hill.

Have you ever wondered why God made you who you are, put you where are, to live in the century when you are? It's because He's got specific stuff for you to do right where you're at *"for such a time as this."* [148] Your street, your school, your workplace, your church, your friendships, your family, your sports, your pastimes, your passions, your talents, your vision, your past, your future, your generation

## THE DARKER THINGS GET, THE BRIGHTER WE GET TO SHINE FOR JESUS.

– it all looks completely different when you realise that it's all part of God's cross-driven purpose for your life. We were saved to shine – like a city on a hill. To let the brilliant light of Jesus blaze out of our lives into the surrounding darkness, giving hope to those who haven't got any. I love how J.K Falconer put it:

*"I have but one candle of life to burn, and I would rather burn it out in a land filled with darkness than in a land flooded with light."*

This world needs Jesus. It needs Him so bad! I don't know why He's put us where we are, and trusted us to show people the way, but I'm stoked that He has. I'm grateful that the darkness is our mission-field, not our destiny. I'm glad that the darker things get, the brighter we get to shine for Jesus.

I'm just buzzing that we've got a reason to live.

I confess that sometimes I feel completely out of my depth as I look around at the immensity of what God has called us to do. Sometimes it feels like it's just too much. That things are too messed-up out there, and that my bit of the world is too dark for me to make any kind of difference. But then I remember Jesus. I remember the never-ending power of His cross. I remember that He's alive, He's compassionate, and He still gets a kick out saving people. I remember that He wins in the end! And all of a sudden the darkness isn't a reason to surrender anymore...

It's a reason to shine.

## 5. Unashamed

*"Nor do people light a lamp and put it under a basket, but on a stand and it gives light to all in the house..."*

The light of our lifestyle is more powerful than I think we'll ever fully know. D.L Moody once said that out of one hundred men, one will read the Bible, the other ninety nine will read the Christian. The apostle Paul said something very similar when he wrote: *"Your very lives are a letter that anyone can read just by looking at you."* [149]

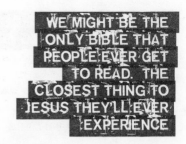

WE MIGHT BE THE ONLY BIBLE THAT PEOPLE EVER GET TO READ. THE CLOSEST THING TO JESUS THEY'LL EVER EXPERIENCE

I find that an incredibly challenging thought.

We might be the only Bible that people ever get to read. The closest thing to Jesus they'll ever experience. Woah! If that's really the case – what kind of impression do they get of Him, based on the evidence of our lives? Do we attract people to Jesus Christ or put them off Him? Like that old saying goes, if being a Christian was a criminal offence, would there even be enough evidence to convict us? Is Jesus elevated in every area of our lives, or have we opted for the comfort of burying Him under a basket?

Do we shine for Jesus, or are we ashamed of Him?

True cross-driven living involves smashing up anything that looks like a basket, and shamelessly lifting Jesus up through our lifestyle, so that anyone who comes near gets to see the sheer brilliance of His gospel light in us.

Jesus has ignited within us His divine, life-giving light – how dare we even think about hiding it under the baskets of cowardice or compromise? Claiming to follow Jesus is pointless if the life-changing power of His gospel is nowhere to be seen in our lives. What credibility do we have if we're completely invisible to the world, or if we've embraced the culture of the world to the extent that we look and live exactly the same as everyone else? Christianity that's anonymous or scandalous isn't revolutionary – it's destructive, as Brennan Manning reminds us:

*"The greatest single cause of atheism in the world today is Christians, who acknowledge Jesus with their lips and walk out the door, and deny Him by their lifestyle. That is what an unbelieving world simply finds unbelievable."* [150]

Can I be blunt here? Hiding behind the doors of the church because you're scared of getting contaminated or persecuted by the people outside is not

## JESUS HAS CALLED US TO BE SET APART, NOT SOLD OUT

putting your lamp on a stand – it's a basket that needs smashing up! Similarly, puffing on spliffs, worshipping wealth or messing around with sex is not putting your lamp on a stand – It's a basket that needs smashing up.

Jesus has called us to be set apart, not sold out.

To be *in* the world, but not *of* it.  To infiltrate and influence the world, but never at the expense of integrity or visibility.  To be contagious for Christ, without compromising His gospel, or cowering from its responsibilities.  To stand up and be counted worthy of the calling we've received. [151]

Paul once wrote: *"You are to live clean, innocent lives as children of God in a dark world full of crooked and perverse people.  Let your lives shine brightly before them."* [152]

The Righteous revolutionaries of Jesus are called to show that there's another way of doing life other than getting loaded, getting laid and getting paid.  That God's got so much more for us than fighting, lying, stealing, gossiping, bullying, boasting and down-loading porn.  We're called to rebel against the currently accepted, broken, soul-destroying way of doing life, and instead live out the full, beautiful reality of the abundant life of Jesus.  To blaze a trail to the Light of Life, living with such revolutionary purity, honesty, humility and integrity that just like moths are drawn to a flame, people will be drawn to Jesus because of what they see in us.

Jesus Himself promised that *"I, when I am lifted up from the earth, will draw all people to myself."* [153]  Therefore as we make Him first in our lives, elevating Him for all to see, and radiating the power and passion of His resurrection life why wouldn't people want a bit of that?

## FRESH START

I can't write about the crucial importance of living radical lives that attract people to Jesus without going off on a little tangent to say some important stuff.  I've got no doubt that there will be people reading this who probably feel that they've really blown it as a Christian. That they've done and said stuff that they shouldn't have and that no one will ever take them seriously as a Christian again. They feel that they'll never fully be able to shine for Jesus again because everyone knows what they've been like, and that the best they'll ever be now is a second-rate Christian. If that's you, can I just encourage you to do two things?

> **WE'RE CALLED TO REBEL AGAINST THE CURRENTLY ACCEPTED, BROKEN, SOUL-DESTROYING WAY OF DOING LIFE, AND INSTEAD LIVE OUT THE FULL, BEAUTIFUL REALITY OF THE ABUNDANT LIFE OF JESUS**

Firstly, recognise that talk like that comes from direct from the devil (a.k.a the father of lies) so you can tell him shut up and give him a spiritual wedgie!

Secondly, take another look at the cross of Jesus – the place where grace and forgiveness flow freely forever, and where fresh starts can always be found by those humble enough to ask for one. Then remember that if He's got to power to rise from the dead, He can certainly turn your situation around!

> **TAKE ANOTHER LOOK AT THE CROSS OF JESUS – THE PLACE WHERE GRACE AND FORGIVENESS FLOW FREELY FOREVER, AND WHERE FRESH STARTS CAN ALWAYS BE FOUND BY THOSE HUMBLE ENOUGH TO ASK FOR ONE**

Can I suggest that you come clean to Jesus about how and when you've messed-up, ask Him to wipe the slate clean, and to give you the wisdom and strength to put things right. You may need to speak with people face-to-face, send out a group text or leave a note on your MySpace or Facebook page, owning up to your failures and asking for forgiveness. Explain that you're committed to living a life that honours Jesus, and that while you're still a work in progress, things are about to change.

Now some people won't have a clue what you're on about and some might think you're nuts! However, I guarantee you that most people will deeply respect you, because that kind of honesty and courage is incredibly rare. And who knows, it may just signal the start of a new chapter in your cross-driven mission, as people to start looking for the light of Jesus in your life.

# 6. Glory

*"In the same way, let your light shine before others, so that they may see your good works and give glory to your Father who is in heaven."*

Mark is very much my right-hand man on the Offensive course. He's a passionate cross-driven missionary, a talented artist and a big source of encouragement to me. However, that's not how it always was...

Mark grew up in Worthing (Southern England). Early on in High School he started using drugs with mates and as he threw himself into the whole drug and music scene his life became increasingly unstable and destructive. One of the ways that Mark used to get his kicks was by being cruel and abusive to a small bunch of Christians whose love for Jesus really wound him up. They were easy targets, and he didn't like them having something he didn't (faith). However, they never retaliated, but rather showed him grace, which wound him up even more!

By the time he was 15, Mark's drug problems had got out of control, and when dealers started chasing him for drug-debts that he couldn't pay, he tried (unsuccessfully) to hang himself. Mark sank deeper into dark depression and didn't know where to turn. It was then that the Christians whose lives he had sought to destroy came alongside him, gave him hope and explained to him how much he was loved by God. Mark was stunned by the way that they were still willing to have anything to do with him, though it was all the evidence He needed to believe in the reality of the Jesus who shone so clearly in their lives. Mark turned to Jesus for forgiveness and new life, and that's exactly what he got.

People can argue till they're blue in the face about whether God's real, or if the Bible's true or not, but as Mark will tell you, no one can argue with the power of a Christ-centred, salt-spreading, light-shedding, cross-driven life of grace and hope.

## OFFENSIVE

Cross-driven living creates a platform for the cross-driven message, and the cross-driven message is authenticated by a cross-driven life.

IF WE WANT TO SEE PEOPLE SAVED – WE NEED TO LIVE LIKE IT!

If we want to see people saved – we need to live like it!

So while it would be great if we only needed to just speak the name of Jesus for people to flock to Him and get saved, the reality is that many today are either skeptical of our message, put off by religious hypocrisy or scared to trust in a God that they can't see or understand. Therefore they watch from a distance, scrutinizing our lives, curious to see if the way that we live backs-up the words we speak. That's why Jesus has commanded us to do whatever it takes to live as righteous revolutionaries. As salt that tastes good and makes people thirsty for Him, and light that pierces the darkness, offering hope to people who are desperate for it.

Whether it takes days, years or even decades of consistent, attractive, Godly living, we need to be praying for that one moment when all of a sudden someone just clicks that the gospel is what lies behind our good news lives, and they ask us to fill in the blanks for them:

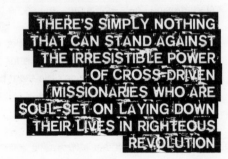
THERE'S SIMPLY NOTHING THAT CAN STAND AGAINST THE IRRESISTIBLE POWER OF CROSS-DRIVEN MISSIONARIES WHO ARE SOUL-SET ON LAYING DOWN THEIR LIVES IN RIGHTEOUS REVOLUTION

*"Be ready to speak up and tell anyone who asks why you're living the way you are."* [154]

Peter also encourages us to:

*"Live such good lives among the pagans that, though they accuse you of doing wrong, they may see your good deeds and glorify God on the day He visits us."* [155]

That's the whole point of living all-out for Jesus. There's simply nothing that can stand against the irresistible power of cross-driven missionaries who are soul-set on laying down their lives in righteous revolution.

So let's rebel to the glory of God.

THE AFTERMATH
STEVE'S STORY

" I used to go to church on a Sunday morning and be the loudest and proudest person there. But when it came to living the Christian lifestyle and going out with my non Christian friends, I was no longer the Loudest and proudest, I didn't mention Jesus and what he had done for me or how he had saved me. It was like I was almost embarrassed to be a Christian outside of Church.

What happened next?

I attended the Offensive course in 2007, and in the Righteous Revolution session I received a slap in the face. No, not a real slap in the face but a spiritual slap. God opened up my heart to his word which was that we are to be unashamed of the Gospel, that we are to be a light shining before all men (Matthew 5v16) and that we are not to hide that Light

After the session I prayed and I felt God saying to me what will you do now?
I decided I was no longer going to hide my light under a bowl. Soon after Offensive I started to talk to my non Christian friends about Jesus one even got saved, I'm still praying for the rest. I also decided I was going to take Jesus into my work place. One thing I have learnt is that actions sometimes speak louder than words, as people often notice what you do or don't do more than what you say.

I guess we don't just tell people about Jesus, we need to show Him to them! "

# CHAPTER SIX

"IF NOT ME, THEN WHO?
IF NOT NOW, THEN WHEN?" [156]

- RABBI HILLEL

PENCIL

As the world's keeps turning and while there's still breath in our nostrils, the biggest, most exciting, most scary, and most important search and

rescue mission in history rolls on, and we're privileged to be part of it.

Jesus has called us to go out into the streets and suburbs, communities and countries, crossing cultures and lines of comfort, in order to shamelessly declare and demonstrate the glorious gospel of Jesus Christ – the hero of heaven who came, who died, who's alive, and who saves to the uttermost! We go with hearts burning with passion for our King, and for the lost people He loves. And we go with our faces bowed to the ground saying *"Jesus – it's all about you. You do the saving and we'll give you all the glory you deserve!"*

As far as I'm concerned, this chapter is the most exciting chapter in the whole book. It's exciting because it's nothing to do with me. It's all yours! My heart's desire is that every single copy of this book will be entirely unique, as whoever reads it whole-heartedly takes up the challenge to play their individual part in the cross-driven mission. We've all got different gifts and different callings, so these final pages are for you to use in whatever way you want. You can write down prayers, scriptures, dreams, challenges or fears. You can draw pictures or diagrams, write down prophetic words, record answered prayers or stories of encouragement. Even the title page has got space for you to give this chapter a name of your own choice.

Mother Teresa once said: *"I am a little pencil in the hand of a writing God who is sending a love letter to the world."*

What's God going to write to the world through you?

I truly pray that God will bless you immensely as you journey with Him on the cross-driven mission of a lifetime.

Take the message.

Change the world.

Go for it…

OFFENSIVE

# OFFENSIVE

# REFERENCES

Abbreviations:

NIV New International Version
NLT New Living Translation
NKJV New King James Version
MSG The Message
NCV New Century Version

## INTRO

1. Galatians 5v11
2. Mark 8v34

## CHAPTER 1

3. Lecrae, Send Me, from the Album 'After The Music Stops', Cross Movement Records, 2006
4. U2, Peace On Earth, from the Album 'All that you can't leave behind', Island Records, 2000
5. Luke 9v10
6. Mark 1v16-18
7. Preached by Andy during the EZ36 launch event in Cardiff, February 2002.
8. Erwin R. MacManus, The Barbarian Way, 2005 Nelson Books, text taken from the back cover
9. John 10v10 [NCV]
10. Mark 8v34-35
11. Mark 10v45
12. Mark 16v15 [NLT]
13. Revelation 5v9 [NLT]
14. Matthew 28v19
15. Keith Green, 'What's Wrong With The Gospel, Section 2 – The Added Parts: http://www.lastdaysministries.org/Articles/1000008643/Last_Days_Ministries/LDM/Last_Days_Magazine/Articles_Archive/Whats_Wrong_With.aspx

16. Acts 1v8 [NLT]
17. Galatians 2v20 [NIV]
18. Philippians 1v21 [NIV]
19. An entry in Jim Elliot's journal
20. Written in a letter in 1740
21. Erwin R. MacManus, The Barbarian Way, 2005 Nelson Books, p.108
22. 2Corinthians 11v23-27 [NLT]
23. Matthew 28v20 [NKJV]
24. Hebrews 13v5
25. Psalm 16v11
26. Nehemiah 8v10

## CHAPTER 2

27. 1Corinthians 9v16
28. Romans 10v13
29. Romans 10v14-15
30. Mark 1v14
31. 1Corinthians 15v1-5
32. Mark 1v1
33. Acts 4v12 [NIV]
34. Jim Elliot, written in a letter to his parents dated June 23, 1947
35. Jewish War 7.203
36. Luke 23v33
37. Romans 3v23 [NLT]
38. Romans 6v23 [NLT]
39. John 3v17 [NLT]
40. 2 Corinthians 5v21 [NIV]
41. Matthew 27v46 [NKJV]
42. Psalm 103v1&10 [NIV]
43. Luke 23v42-43 [NIV]
44. Luke 23v34 [NLT]
45. Psalm 51v4 [NLT]
46. Psalm 103v12 [NLT]
47. Hebrews 10v22 [NIV]
48. 1John1v7
49. "Oh, for a Thousand Tongues to Sing" by Charles Wesley, 1707-1788

50. http://www.independent.co.uk/news/world/middle-east/in-his-own-words-alan-johnston-on-his-release-456010.html
51. Mark 10v45[NLT]
52. John 19v30 [NKJV]
53. R.E.M, Everybody Hurts, from the Album 'Automatic For The People', Warner Bros, 1992
54. Isaiah 53v5 [NIV]
55. Romans 5v8 [NIV]
56. 1John 4v16
57. 1Corinthians 15v14 [NKJV]
58. Isaiah 59v14 [NKJV]
59. John 18v38
60. Mark 8v31 [NIV]
61. 1Corinthians 15v55&57
62. John 14v2 [NLT]
63. Revelation 21v2-4
64. Mark 1v15
65. Ephesians 4v15
66. Ali G in interview with Tomasz Starzewski on Ali G "Innit", 1999
67. A good example of this in the Bible is 1Thessalonians 1v9
68. 1 Corinthians 1v22-24 [NIV]
69. Romans 5v6 [NIV]

## CHAPTER 3

70. C.H Spurgeon, Daniel: A Pattern For Pleaders," the Metropolitan Tabernacle, Pulpit, vol 61 (1915), from the C.H. Spurgeon Collection
71. Mark 1v35-39 [MSG]
72. John Piper, 'Let the Nations be glad: The Supremacy of God in Mission', Grand Rapids: Baker, 2003, p.41
73. David McCasland, 'Oswald Chambers: Abandoned to God: The Life Story of the Author of My Utmost for His Highest', Discovery House Publishers, 1998, p.110
74. Matthew 6v6 [NKJV]
75. Matthew 6v9-13 [NKJV]
76. John 14v6 [NLT]
77. Galatians 4v5-7 [NLT]

78. Psalm 103v8
79. Psalm 68v5 [NIV]
80. Jonah 2v9
81. Zephania 3v17 [NIV]
82. 2Corinthians 12v9 [NLT]
83. C.H Spurgeon, Daniel: A Pattern For Pleaders," the Metropolitan Tabernacle, Pulpit, vol 61 (1915), from the C.H. Spurgeon Collection
84. Judges 21v25 [NIV]
85. Psalm 45v6 [NIV]
86. John 3v3 [NIV]
87. Available for free at www.igniteme.org
88. 1Thessaloninans 5v17
89. Tears quote: Tim Chester and Steve Timmis, Total Church: A Radical Reshaping Around Gospel and Community, Inter Varsity Press, 2007, p.143
90. Luke 19v41
91. Psalm 126v5 [NIV]
92. Matthew 17v22-23 [NIV]
93. John 6v38
94. John 5v19 [NLT]
95. John 12v49-50 [NLT]
96. John Piper, Prayer: The Power of Christian Hedonism: http://www.desiringgod.org/ResourceLibrary/Sermons/ByDate/1983/410_Prayer_The_Power_of_Christian_Hedonism/
97. Matthew 7v9-11 [NIV]
98. Philippians 4v19 [MSG]
99. Isaiah 59v1-2 [NIV]
100. Delirious? "Our God reigns, from album "Mission Bell, 2005
101. 2Chronicles 7v14 [NKJV]
102. 1John 1v8
103. Matthew 5v44
104. 1Peter 5v8 [NIV]
105. Hebrews 4v15-16 [NIV]
106. Anonymous

## CHAPTER 4

107. 2Corinthians 5v14 [NKJV]
108. www.wikipedia.org/wiki/Fire
109. Dictionary According to Dai, 2007
110. Jeremiah 20v9 [NLT]
111. Song of Songs 8v6 [NLT]
112. Matthew 22v36 [NKJV]
113. Matthew 22v38-40 [NKJV]
114. John Stott, Romans: God's Good News for the World, Downers Grover, Inter-Varsity, 1994, 53.
115. Matt Redman, Mission's Flame, from the Album 'Face Down', Survivor, 2004
116. Psalm 31v23
117. John 14v15 [NCV]
118. Colossians 1v21 [NKJV]
119. Luke 7v47 [NLT]
120. 1John 4v19 [NKJV]
121. Genesis 2v7 [NLT]
122. John 4v24
123. Mark 12v30 [NIV]
124. James 2v8
125. Jonah 4v11 [NKJV]
126. Erwin R. MacManus, The Barbarian Way, 2005 Nelson Books, p.14
127. Luke 10v37
128. Luke 22v42
129. 1 Corinthians 13v4-8 [MSG]

## CHAPTER 5

130. Delirious?, Now Is The Time, taken from album 'The Mission Bell, Furious?, 2005
131. John 14v6
132. Luke 4v18-19 [NKJV]
133. Ephesians 2v9
134. Romans 10v17

135. Psalm 34v8

136. A phrase coined by Shane Claiborne in his book 'The Irresistible Revolution'.

137. Matthew 5v13-16

138. John 4v13&14

139. Matthew 5v6

140. There's a character on South Park called Mr.Hankey The Christmas Poo – a piece of talking poo that comes out of the toilet at Christmas.

141. www.compassionuk.org

142. Proverbs 4v19 [NIV]

143. 1John 1v5

144. John 8v12

145. Psalm 50v2a [NLT]

146. Psalm 50v2b [NLT]

147. 1Peter 2v9

148. Esther 4v14

149. 2Corinthians 3v3 [MSG]

150. Brennan Manning, quoted in the prelude to the DC Talk song 'What If I Stumble?' on the album: Jesus Freak, ForeFront Records, 1995

151. Ephesians 4v10 [NIV]

152. Philippians 2v15 [NLT]

153. John 12v32

154. 1Peter 3v15 [MSG]

155. 1Peter 2v12 [NIV]

## CHAPTER 6

156. Contemporary paraphrase of 1st Century Jewish Rabbi Hillel's quote: "If I am not for myself, who will be for me? And when I am for myself, what am 'I'? And if not now, when?" [Pirkei Avot 1:14]

**OFFENSIVE**

# ignite

## DECLARATION

I believe that God has a special purpose for my generation and me.
I ask God to ignite in me a desire to discover this purpose.

## I COMMIT TO:

* **include** Jesus in my moral life, my thoughts, words, actions and relationships.

* **grow** closer to Jesus through studying the Bible, praying and allowing the Holy Spirit to lead me each day.

* **network** with other Christians in my city, my country and throughout the world.

* **involve** myself in a local church and respect its leadership.

* **take** the message of Jesus into my school, college or place of work and the world by praying, living and witnessing so that everyone may have an opportunity to know Jesus.

* **explore** God's will for myself and my generation and seek to follow it.

---

For further information contact:

Ignite
PO Box 39
Dinas Powys
South Wales   CF64 4ZX

T:   029 20 512247
E:   info@igniteme.org
E:   Dai Hankey: dai@igniteme.org
W:   www. igniteme.org